It's Your Choice

A Personal Guide to
Birth Control Methods for Women
...and Men Too!

Robert A. Hatcher, MD
Nancy Josephs
Felicia H. Stewart, MD
Felicia J. Guest
Gary K. Stewart, MD
Deborah Kowal

 Irvington Publishers, Inc.
551 Fifth Avenue, New York, NY 10176

Copyright © 1982 by Irvington Publishers Inc.

Library of Congress Cataloging in Publication Data
Main entry under title:

It's your choice.

  Bibliography.
  Includes index.
  1. Contraceptives. 2. Contraception.
I. Hatcher, Robert Anthony, 1937-
RG137.I87   1982   613.9'4   82-4678
ISBN 0-8290-0546-3

Printed in the United States of America.

AUTHORS

ROBERT A. HATCHER, M.D., M.P.H., F.A.A.P., has directed the Emory University/Grady Memorial Hospital Family Planning Program since 1968. He is associate professor of Gynecology and Obstetrics at the Emory University School of Medicine in Atlanta, Georgia. He is the senior author of *Contraceptive Technology.* This basic textbook for physicians, medical students, family planning counselors, and nurse practitioners is now in its 11th edition and has sold more than 800,000 copies. He is also an author of *My Body, My Health* and *Contraceptive Technology: Africa.* He is the recipient of the 1981 Rockefeller Public Service Award for Distinguished Service to Families and Youth. He is active in his local church and community, where he and his wife Carolyn often conduct sex education programs for parents and teens. He is an enthusiastic tennis player and gardener.

NANCY JOSEPHS, B.A., is a graduate of the University of Michigan where she majored in political science. She spent six months in London researching constituency and parliamentary issues for a Member of Parliament, as well as successfully running his campaign for reelection. She worked at Emory University Family Planning Program and the Planned Parenthood affiliate of Atlanta. She is an author of the most recent edition of *Contraceptive Technology.* She is currently attending Columbia University, School of Public Health working towards her masters in public health. She loves tennis, racquetball, swimming, and photography.

FELICIA H. STEWART, M.D., practices obstetrics and gynecology in Sacramento, California. She is a clinical lecturer in Obstetrics and Gynecology at the University of California School of Medicine in Davis California. She is senior author of *My Body, My Health,* and an author of *Contraceptive Technology* and *Contraceptive Technology: Africa.* She has published clinical research based on her eight years' work with the Planned Parenthood Association of Sacramento, and is an active public speaker on women's health care issues. She enjoys her children, racquetball, and music.

FELICIA J. GUEST, B.A. develops and conducts training courses at the Regional Training Center for Family Planning, Emory University School

v

of Medicine, Atlanta, Georgia. For six years she wrote and produced patient education materials as the health educator with the Emory University/Grady Memorial Hospital Family Planning Program. She has written *To Comfort and Relieve Them*, a manual for counseling rape victims, and writes a bimonthly health education newsletter for the National Clearinghouse for Family Planning Information. She is an author of *Contraceptive Technology* and *My Body, My Health*. She plays the clarinet and believes the Atlanta Braves will win a pennant in her lifetime.

GARY K. STEWART, M.D., M.P.H., F.A.C.O.G., practices obstetrics and gynecology in Sacramento, California. He is medical director of the Planned Parenthood Association of Sacramento, and assistant clinical professor of Obstetrics and Gynecology at the University of California School of Medicine in Davis, California. He is an author of *Contraceptive Technology, Contraceptive Technology: Africa* and *My Body, My Health*. He was a Peace Corps physician for three years in East Africa, and his interests include African art and photography.

DEBORAH KOWAL, PA-C, is the editor of *Contraceptive Technology Update*, a newsletter for health professionals, the associate editor of the *Epidemiology Monitor*, and a co-author of *Contraceptive Technology: Africa*. Prior to moving to Atlanta, Georgia, she had been a practicing physician's assistant at the University of Michigan Health Service in Ann Arbor. A devoted exerciser, she enjoys backpacking and camping.

YOU CAN BE AN AUTHOR TOO
An Invitation to Individuals or Groups
Providing Health Counseling or Peer Group Counseling Services

Irvington Publishers is interested in publishing brief regional supplements to accompany *It's Your Choice*. If you are interested in preparing a regional or local supplement which would include, for example, names and addresses of local resources for birth control information, please write to Irvington Publishers, Inc., 551 Fifth Avenue, New York, New York 10176.

HOW TO USE THIS BOOK

IT'S YOUR CHOICE is a book to be used as well as read. You will find information about the different birth control methods: what are good choices for you (for now and for later), what are the advantages and disadvantages of each method, and how to use the method you choose as safely as possible. IT'S YOUR CHOICE is a book of self-assessment questionnaires and instructions. You won't learn everything there is to know about health care, but you will learn a great deal more about an important part of your health: how to use birth control methods safely and effectively—and with understanding. And if you wish to know more, this book is an excellent introduction to a whole library of books on your health.

We especially recommend that you read Chapter 1 of this book. Choosing a birth control method involves more than picking the most effective, or the most convenient, method. The correct method for you depends on your health, your lifestyle, your feelings about a particular method, the availability of medical care, and many other factors. In Chapter 1, you will see how the different methods compare. On page 13, you will learn how to develop your own "Reproductive Life Plan"—an important plan in choosing the birth control method that best fits the way you live now and the way you hope to live in the future. On page 15, you will find questions to ask yourself, specific questions about the method you may be thinking of using, or may already be using, to find out if you truly feel comfortable about the method.

The rest of the chapters in the book offer more in-depth information about each of the birth control methods. How do you use the method? What are some of the causes of accidental pregnancy? "Tips for Success" help you use the method effectively. And "warning signals" help you use the method safely. You can read the whole book, especially if you are just deciding what method to use, or you can turn to the specific chapter describing the method you have already chosen.

IF YOU USE PILLS, go to page 29.

IF YOU USE A DIAPHRAGM, go to page 56.

IF YOU USE AN IUD, go to page 48.

IF YOU USE CONDOMS, go to page 64.

IF YOU USE ANY OTHER METHOD, go to the table of contents to find where your method is described in detail.

When it comes to the important decision of whether or when, to have children and what birth control method is best for you, remember, IT'S YOUR CHOICE. We hope this book will help you choose well.

CONTENTS

xi

See Your Clinician Or Go To An Emergency Room
Tips For Success

CHAPTER 1: CHOOSING A BIRTH CONTROL METHOD
Effectiveness, safety, and other important considerations

This is a book about your freedom to choose. It is about your freedom to choose whether or not to have intercourse, whether or not to have children, and whether or not to use birth control, have an abortion, or have a sterilization operation.

For centuries the ability of women to make these choices has been limited by laws, taboos, and medical policies. The result is that women in the past were denied the freedom to choose the course of their own reproductive destiny. Thankfully, times have changed. Women today have the right—and the responsibility—to make very important reproductive decisions.

INTERCOURSE

One of our basic freedoms is the right to choose NOT to have intercourse. However, not everyone *feels* free to make this decision. Freedom is limited if marriage occurs at a very young age, if there is incest, if there is rape, or if there is very strong pressure from parents or friends.

There are areas of the world today where marriage at ages 12, 13, 14, and 15 is very common. In our society pressures are different. Young people are pressured to have early INTERCOURSE rather than early MARRIAGE. Television, movies, popular songs, and advertising campaigns glorify sex. Sometimes friends pressure teens to have intercourse. And sometimes a teen pressures him- or herself. Another might try to impress friends by being "the first" to have intercourse. If a young woman, or an older one feels unloved, she might believe that having intercourse would fill the void that troubles her.

CHILDREN

Another of our basic freedoms is the right to choose when, or if, we want to have children. For couples to be free to make these choices, they

1

must be free to choose whether or not they will use a modern method of birth control. Most women who come to a family planning clinic or to a private doctor's office for birth control have two concerns uppermost in their minds. They want a method of birth control that is *effective,* and they want a method of birth control that is *safe.* This chapter will discuss the methods available, and will help you compare safety, effectiveness, and other important factors. This information will help you use your freedom to choose as wisely as possible.

METHODS OF BIRTH CONTROL

Before I went to the family planning clinic I thought the only good method was the Pill. They sure opened my eyes about lots of other methods.
—woman, age 20

There are several good birth control methods for couples who want to have intercourse without pregnancy:

- Pills
- Mini-Pills
- IUDs
- Diaphragms
- Vaginal Spermicides
- Condoms
- Fertility Awareness Methods

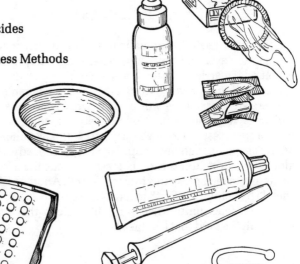

Figure 1:1 Several methods of birth control which are available in the United States today.

Other options are also covered in this book: abstinence, for those who choose not to have intercourse; withdrawal and "morning-after" methods—two emergency options; abortion, for those who have an unplanned pregnancy; and sterilization, for those who are sure they want no more pregnancies in the future. What follows is a quick introduction to the seven most popular temporary methods. Are you ready to start thinking about *your choices?*

PILLS: Two manufactured chemicals mimic the effect of a woman's own hormones, estrogen and progesterone. Taking the Pill every 24 hours prevents ovulation. That means the woman's body does not ripen and release any eggs from her overies, and no egg—no pregnancy.

MINI-PILLS: One manufactured chemical mimics the effect of a woman's own hormone progesterone. Taking a Mini-Pill every day can prevent ovulation in many women. It also thickens the mucus that is produced in the entrance to the uterus, so it is difficult for sperm to enter the uterus.

IUDs: An IUD placed inside the hollow cavity of a woman's uterus probably prevents a fertilized egg from attaching to the wall of the uterus at the beginning of pregnancy. This small piece of plastic is placed inside the uterus by a doctor or a nurse practitioner.

DIAPHRAGMS: This shallow rubber cup is covered with sperm-killing jelly or cream and inserted in the vagina before intercourse. The diaphragm keeps sperm away from the uterus, and the jelly or cream kills any sperm that get near the opening to the uterus.

VAGINAL SPERMICIDES: Foams, creams, jellies, and suppositories all work the same way. They are inserted in the vagina before intercourse, blocking the opening to the uterus. Chemicals contained in the spermicides kill sperm.

CONDOMS: A condom is a latex rubber sheath placed over the erect penis before intercourse. It prevents sperm from coming in contact with the woman's body, because when the man ejaculates, or comes, his semen stays inside the condom.

FERTILITY AWARENESS METHODS: Couples who use these techniques keep careful records of the woman's monthly fertility cycles. They use these records to learn when to avoid intercourse or when to use a method of birth control.

How well do these methods work?
How safe are they?
What would it feel like to use them?

Keep reading.... The answers to these questions follow.

3

EFFECTIVENESS:
HOW WELL DOES THE METHOD WORK?

"Which is the most effective method?"
"Which do you think would be the most effective method for me?"
"Why did one doctor tell me diaphragms were 98% effective and another say they were 87% effective?"
"Will the method I'm considering really work?"

Most couples will not bother with a method of birth control unless they think it will work to prevent pregnancy. This table shows the failure rates for the most popular methods of birth control.

FIRST-YEAR FAILURE RATES OF BIRTH CONTROL· METHODS

	Lowest Observed Failure Rate* (%)	Failure Rate in Typical Users** (%)
Tubal ligation	0.04	0.04
Vasectomy	0.15	0.15
Combined birth control Pills	0.5	2.0
Mini-Pills	1.0	2.5
IUD	1.5	4.0
Condom	2.0	10.0
Diaphragm (with spermicides)	2.0	13.0
Vaginal spermicides: foams, creams, jellies, and suppositories	3-5	15.0
Withdrawal	16.0	23.0
Fertility awareness methods: basal body temperature, mucus method, calendar, and "rhythm"	2-20	20-30
Douche	—	40.0
Chance (no method of birth control)	90.0	90.0

*Designed to complete the sentence: "Of 100 women who start out the year using this method, and who use it correctly and consistently, the lowest observed failure rate has been ____ by the end of the year."
**Designed to complete the sentence: "Of 100 typical women who start out the year using this method, the number who will be pregnant by the end of the year will be ____."

References to this table can be found in Appendix 3.

4

As you can see, *all* the methods *can be* very good protection. You can also see that *the more careful you are, the better the method works for you.* For example, Pills are very effective, yet a lot of Pill users become pregnant because *they don't use Pills carefully and correctly.* Your job is to choose a method you believe you can use correctly *all the time.*

What would you do if you had an unplanned pregnancy? What are your attitudes about abortion? About adoption? About raising a child as a single parent? Because the failure rates vary from method to method, try to be honest with yourself when thinking about your choices. Only you can assess your values and thoughts. If having an abortion is an acceptable option for you, you might choose a method that has slightly lower effectiveness rates, such as the condom or vaginal spermicides. On the other hand, if you are completely uncomfortable with the idea of an abortion, you might use a method with higher effectiveness rates, such as Pills or the IUD, or you might use *two* contraceptives at the same time, such as condoms and foam together.

**ANY TWO METHODS USED TOGETHER
WILL GIVE YOU MORE PROTECTION THAN EITHER WILL ALONE**

SAFETY

Just as no contraceptive is 100% effective, no contraceptive is without risk. There are a variety of risks you might encounter with any method of birth control. Fortunately, most of these risks are not common. First, there are risks related to the *dangers of the method* itself. How often might the method be associated with death, hospitalization, loss of fertility, pain, or infection? Second, there are inconvenience problems. Does the method make sexual intercourse less pleasant? Does it cause nagging irritations such as nausea, irregular periods, or vaginal burning? Finally, there are risks associated with *pregnancy* should the method fail. What are the dangers of pregnancy to you personally? Would pregnancy disrupt your life in a major way?

The concept of *risks and benefits* is extremely important to keep in mind when you choose your method of birth control. There are several good ways of thinking of the risks and benefits of a method:

Risks	Benefits
Bad News	Good News
Disadvantages of the method	Advantages of the method
Complications	Side-Benefits

5

In the next section the risks and benefits for each method of birth control are outlined in some detail.

The most serious risk of birth control is death, but that risk is very low. When considering the risks associated with a method of birth control it

---

Voluntary Risks In Perspective

Activity	Chance of Death in a Year
Motorcycling	1 in 50
Smoking, 1 pack per day	1 in 200
Horse racing	1 in 200
Automobile driving	1 in 6,000
Power boating	1 in 6,000
Rock climbing	1 in 7,500
Playing football	1 in 25,000
Canoeing	1 in 100,000
Using tampons	1 in 350,000
Using birth control Pills (nonsmoker)	1 in 63,000
Using birth control Pills (smoker)	1 in 16,000
Using IUDs	1 in 100,000
Using diaphragm, condom, or spermicide	None
Using fertility awareness methods	None
Undergoing sterilization:	
laparoscopic tubal ligation	1 in 10,000
hysterectomy	1 in 1,600
vasectomy	None
Pregnancy:	
continuing pregnancy	1 in 10,000
illegal abortion	1 in 3,000
legal abortion	
before 9 weeks	1 in 400,000
between 9-12 weeks	1 in 100,000
between 13-16 weeks	1 in 25,000
after 16 weeks	1 in 10,000

REFERENCES:

Dinman, B.D.: "The reality and acceptance of risk," *JAMA* 244:1226-28, 1980.

Tietze, C.: "New estimates of mortality associated with fertility control," *Fam Plan Perspect* 9:74-76, 1977.

National Center for Health Statistics, *Final Mortality Statistics, United States, 1976-1978*.

Centers for Disease Control: *Abortion-related Mortality, United States, 1976-1978*.

can be helpful to think about the risks of other daily or common activities. The preceding table, developed by Dr. Willard Cates of the U.S. Centers for Disease Control in Atlanta, describes some of the voluntary risks of life. This information help you compare risks of birth control to other voluntary risks in life.

Here are the benefits and risks of the methods of birth control. Remember that you may never experience any of the risks, nor *all* of the benefits of your method.

COMBINED PILLS
Benefits:
- 99.5% effective if used correctly all the time
- 98% effective with average amount of carefulness
- light, regular periods
- few or no menstrual cramps
- premenstrual problems decreased or absent
- unlikely to develop cysts of the breast or ovary
- no interruption at time of lovemaking
- unlikely to develop anemia (iron-poor blood)
- may improve acne
- less likely to develop rheumatoid arthritis
- may reduce your risk of developing cancer of the uterus and ovaries
- may decrease your risk of developing pelvic infection

Serious Risks:
- increased risk of heart attack, stroke, and other circulatory problems. This *risk applies mostly to Pill users over 35 years and Pill users who smoke*. In a year, circulatory problem deaths among Pill users average 1.8/100,000 for nonsmokers and 6.5/100,000 for smokers.
- liver tumors. Associated with using Pills for more than five years, liver tumors cause only three or four deaths per million Pill users per year. They are very rare.
- cancer. The long-term effects of Pills are *still not known*, but so far, there is no evidence that Pills cause cancer.
- high blood pressure. In most cases, the pressure returns to normal once Pills are stopped.

Bothersome Side Effects (experience has shown that about 4 out of 10 Pill users will have one or more of these side effects):
- headaches
- fluid retention. This problem can cause mild weight gain or breast tenderness. Contact lenses may not fit.
- nausea
- spotting or light bleeding

7

- depression (can be a serious problem)
- may interfere with other medicine (check with your doctor)
- decreased sex drive
- chloasma. Skin darkens on upper lip, forehead, and under the eyes.
- must remember to take Pill *on schedule* every day
- cannot use when breast-feeding

MINI-PILLS

Many experts believe Mini-Pills are safer than regular birth control pills. First, because Mini-Pills contain only one hormone, while regular pills have two. Second, Mini-Pills have a very low dose of hormone. However, since Mini-Pills are fairly new, less is known about them. For now, the Food and Drug Administration recommends that we assume Mini-Pills have the same risks as regular Pills. *So read the combined (regular) Pill information first.* What follows are some benefits and risks that make Mini-Pills *different* from regular Pills.

Benefits:
- 99% effective if used correctly all the time
- 97.5% effective with average amount of carefulness
- probably no interference with breast-feeding
- SEE LIST FOR COMBINED PILLS

Serious Risks:
- increased risk of ectopic pregnancy. Pregnancy occurs in the fallopian tube rather than in the uterus. Requires emergency surgery.
- SEE LIST FOR COMBINED PILLS

Bothersome Side Effects:
- irregular periods
- SEE LIST FOR COMBINED PILLS

IUDs

Benefits:
- 98.5% effective if used correctly all the time
- 96% effective with average amount of carefulness
- no interference at time of lovemaking
- no equipment to keep track of
- nothing to do except check strings and watch for danger signs.
- continuous protection
- no interference with breast-feeding

8

Serious Risks:
- infection of sex organs (uterus, tubes, and/or ovaries) called Pelvic Inflammatory Disease or PID. IUD users have 3 to 9 times more PID than users of other methods. PID can cause serious illness and permanent loss of fertility. Infection during a pregnancy that occurs with an IUD in the uterus can be very serious or even fatal.
- miscarriage. About half of all pregnancies that occur among women using an IUD end in miscarriage. About 25% will miscarry if the IUD is removed.
- ectopic pregnancy. Pregnancy begins in the fallopian tubes rather than the uterus. Requires emergency surgery.
- perforation. The IUD or its inserter punctures the uterus. This happens 1 to 9 times per 1000 insertions and may require surgery to remove the IUD.
- expulsion. IUDs can come out without the user knowing it, which can lead to pregnancy.

Bothersome Side Effects:
- heavy periods
- painful periods
- more likely to develop anemia (iron-poor blood)
- more likely to develop infection of the cervix
- pain at time of IUD insertion or removal

DIAPHRAGM
Benefits:
- 98% effective if used correctly all the time
- 87% effective if used with average amount of carefulness
- no hormone changes in your body
- use only when needed
- does not cause serious medical problems
- need not cause interruption at time of lovemaking
- less likely to develop sexually transmissible infections
- no interference with breast-feeding
- may protect against cancer of the cervix

Serious Risks:
- one study has suggested an increased risk of birth defects among women who use sperm-killing chemicals such as diaphragm cream or jelly. Future studies will help us know whether or not there is a true increased risk.

Bothersome Side Effects:
- allergy to sperm-killing chemicals

9

- uncomfortable pressure from diaphragm rim
- bladder infections
- partner may feel diaphragm during intercourse, especially if diaphragm is too small
- taste of jelly or cream may interfere with oral sex

CONDOMS
Benefits:
- 98% effective if used correctly
- 90% effective if used with average amount of carefulness
- use only when needed
- allows partner to help with birth control
- excellent protection against sexually transmissible infections
- no hormone or chemical changes in your body
- does not cause serious medical problems
- does not interfere with breast-feeding
- may protect against cancer of the cervix
- may be less expensive than other methods
- no doctor or clinic visit is required; available in drugstores
- helpful for men who would like to last longer before ejaculation

Serious Risks:
- NONE

Bothersome Side Effects:
- must be put on just before intercourse
- dulls sensation for some men
- dry condoms may cause irritation for women unless extra lubrication is added

VAGINAL SPERMICIDES (This category includes foam, cream, jelly, and suppositories. These are for birth control, not hygiene.)
Benefits:
- 95-98% effective if used correctly all the time
- 85% effective if used with average amount of carefulness
- use only when needed
- may protect against sexually transmissible infections
- does not cause serious medical problems
- does not interfere with breast-feeding
- may protect against cancer of the cervix
- no doctor or clinic visit required; available in drugstores
- adds lubrication for intercourse

Serious Risks:
- one study has suggested an increased risk of birth defects among women who use spermicides. Future studies will help us know whether or not there is a true increased risk.

Bothersome Side Effects:
- allergy to sperm-killing chemicals
- taste of product may interfere with oral sex
- must be used just before intercourse

FERTILITY AWARENESS METHODS
Benefits:
- 80-98% effective if used correctly all the time
- 70-80% effective if used with average amount of carefulness
- completely safe
- inexpensive
- acceptable to religions that do not approve of other methods
- opportunity to "tune in" to cyclic changes
- may open up new options for nonintercourse, sexual pleasures
- very helpful for planning pregnancy

Serious Risks:
- there is some concern that women who do become pregnant while using this method could have an increased risk of birth defects. If a couple delays intercourse until they believe the fertile time is over, the egg that is fertilized may be "old." Old eggs may be associated with birth defects.

Bothersome Side Effects:
- may limit opportunities for spontaneous intercourse
- difficult to use for women with very irregular cycles
- requires careful record-keeping every day
- must keep records for several cycles before relying on the method
- some women dislike checking vaginal discharge changes
- in the beginning, requires quite a bit of teaching from a counselor

WITHDRAWAL
Benefits:
- 84% effective if used exactly right all the time
- 77% effective if used with average amount of carefulness
- safe
- free
- always available

Serious Risks:
- **NONE**

Bothersome Side Effects:
- requires a good deal of control during intercourse
- not all men know when they are going to ejaculate
- sperm may leave penis even before ejaculation
- not as satisfying for most men and women as ejaculating in the vagina

ABSTINENCE
Benefits:
- 100% effective if used correctly all the time
- far less effective for most users
- safe
- free
- may open up new options for nonintercourse, sexual pleasures
- compatible with value system of many people, especially teenagers

Serious Risks:
- **NONE**

Bothersome Side Effects
- often difficult to stick to decision to abstain

In an effort to decrease the possibility of risks from a given method of birth control, there are certain things a woman can do. Most important, she can decide whether or not it is wise even to consider using a method of birth control. Because some women are more likely to have problems with one method of birth control rather than others, the *contraindications* to methods are important to consider as you make your birth control choice.

A contraindication is a medical condition that could make the use of a method unsafe when it might otherwise be recommended. There are three types of contraindications:
- **ABSOLUTE** contraindications: you **MUST NOT** use the method.
- **STRONG RELATIVE** contraindications: you would be strongly advised not to use the method.
- **OTHER RELATIVE** contraindications: you may be able to try the method if you are willing to be followed very carefully by your doctor or nurse practitioner so that you are watched for early signs of trouble.

Many of the serious complications of Pills and IUDs could be avoided by *paying closer attention to the contraindications* of these methods. Contraindications are explained in detail in the following chapters. Read them carefully for the methods you are considering.

FEELINGS AND LIFE-STYLE

What I want to know is, will *I* like the method? And will *he* like it?
—Woman, age 21

So far we have discussed two considerations that may help you decide what method of birth control you want to use: effectiveness and safety. There are two other important factors to keep in mind when you decide on a method of birth control you want to use: your feelings and your life-style.

How much time do you spend developing a plan for yourself when it comes to sex, birth control, deciding when and if to start a family, and determining how you want children—or the absence of children—to fit into your long-term goals? Your life-style includes your plans about children, how often you have intercourse, the availability of medical care, your ability to pay for birth control, and the amount of cooperation with birth control that you can expect from your partner. This is sometimes called a *reproductive life plan*.

> **EVERY PERSON NEEDS A REPRODUCTIVE LIFE PLAN!**

REPRODUCTIVE LIFE PLAN

Birth control must fit into your reproductive life plan. Ask yourself these questions to help you work out your personal reproductive life plan:

Would I like to have children one day? _____

Would I like to be married one day? _____

How old would I like to be when I have my first child? _____

How many children would I like to have? _____

How sad would I be if I were not able to have *any* children _____

How concerned would I be if I were to become pregnant before I were married? _____

If I were to become pregnant before I wanted to become pregnant, would I consider an abortion? _____

Would I like to wait until I'm married to start having sexual intercourse? _____

How many years of formal education would I like to complete? ____

At what point during or after my education would I like to be married? _____

Would I like to work when my children are toddlers? When my children are in their childhood years? When my children are no longer in the home? _____

Of all the things I could do in my life, probably the most important for me to accomplish is this: _____

Children would affect this goal in the following ways: _____

What would it mean to me if my marriage were to end in divorce? ___

Would I like to have intercourse with the person I marry *before* marriage? _____

How does my life plan fit in with my ethical or religious beliefs? ____

How do I feel about having intercourse with someone other than my spouse? _____

How do I feel about my spouse having intercourse with someone else? _____

How often will I have intercourse? _____

Might I have intercourse with several different partners? _____

These are very personal questions, important in choosing the best method for *you*. Frequent intercourse or intercourse with a number of different partners may make condoms, foam or the diaphragm seem fairly inconvenient to you. Infrequent intercourse might mean you do not want to expose yourself to the daily risks of Pills or an IUD. The risk of infection with more than one partner would be a big consideration in choosing an IUD, especially if you hope to have children at some point in the future.

The questions listed above are repeated in Appendix 5. Your partner may want to answer them in order to find the best method for him or her. Or, you may want to review your reproductive life plan at a future time.

You might also consider the ease with which you can get medical care. IUDs or Pills might be poor choices if you cannot get medical care easily and quickly if serious problems do occur; Mini-Pills might be a better choice in view of their relative safety.

How much can you afford to pay for contraceptives? You need to know in advance what the ongoing expenses for your method will be. Pills may be available free from public family planning clinics, or at a nominal fee, such as one or two dollars per pack, compared with six to eight dollars per pack in some drugstores. It may be a good idea to discuss cost with your partner.

How much cooperation will you be able to count on from your partner? Some methods are impossible to use without your partner's cooperation. Condoms, foam, and even the diaphragm might fit into this category.

IN THE BEST OF ALL POSSIBLE WORLDS, WOMEN
AND MEN SHOULD CHOOSE THE BEST CONTRACEPTIVE TOGETHER;
PAY FOR CONTRACEPTIVE EXPENSES TOGETHER; AND,
WATCH FOR CONTRACEPTIVE DANGER SIGNALS TOGETHER.

FEELINGS ABOUT BIRTH CONTROL: A SELF-ASSESSMENT QUESTIONNAIRE FOR INDIVIDUALS CONSIDERING USE OF A SPECIFIC METHOD OF BIRTH CONTROL
(for women and men considering their contraceptive options)

BACKGROUND: For each method of birth control there is a rate of failure, or a rate of pregnancies, which may occur even if that method of birth control is used perfectly. Since you will be using your method of birth control to avoid an unplanned pregnancy, you want to get just as low a pregnancy rate as possible. You want to be able to use your method CORRECTLY and CONSISTENTLY every time. Obviously, the rate of pregnancies, or failure rate, goes up if for any reason you don't use the method or if you fail to use it exactly as it was designed to be used. The following questions were developed to help you decide if the method you are considering is a good choice or a poor choice for you.

METHOD OF BIRTH CONTROL YOU ARE CONSIDERING USING: _____
Have you had problems using this method before? Yes ____ No ____
How long did you use this method? _____

PLEASE ASK YOURSELF THESE QUESTIONS:

	YES	NO
Am I afraid of using this method?	___	___
Would I really rather *not* use this method?	___	___
Will I have trouble remembering to use this method?	___	___
Have I ever become pregnant while using this method?	___	___
Will I have trouble using this method correctly?	___	___
Do I still have unanswered questions about this method?	___	___
Does this method make menstrual periods longer or more painful?	___	___
Does this method cost more than I can afford?	___	___
Is this method known to have serious complications?	___	___
Am I opposed to this method because of any religious beliefs?	___	___
Is my partner opposed to this method?	___	___
Am I using this method without my partner's knowledge?	___	___
Will using this method embarrass my partner?	___	___
Will using this method embarrass me?	___	___
Will I enjoy intercourse less because of this method?	___	___
Will this method interrupt lovemaking?	___	___
Has a nurse or doctor ever told me **NOT** to use this method?	___	___
Is there anything about my personality that could lead me to use this method incorrectly?	___	___

TOTAL NUMBER OF YES ANSWERS: ___

Most individuals will have a few **yes** answers. **Yes** answers mean that potential problems may lie in store. If you have more than a few **yes** responses, you may want to discuss some of these with your physician, counselor, partner, or friend. Talking it over can help you to decide whether to use this method, or how to use it so it will really be effective for you. In general, *the more yes answers you have, the less likely you are to use this method consistently and correctly.*

This self-assessment questionnaire is repeated 4 times in Appendix 5. Your or your partner may want to use these when considering a new or different method of birth control.

INFORMED CONSENT

A voluntary decision—free from pressure of any kind—is an essential ingredient in choosing a method. As a potential user of a method of birth control, you have a right to know all the information there is to know regarding a method BEFORE you begin using it. For example, if you were considering taking the combined birth control Pill, you should be informed of the Pill's possible side effects, benefits, and risks. This information can be provided by doctors, nurses, family planning counselors, and health educators. It is necessary in order for you to make a truly *informed choice.* Make sure you receive the following information:

- A full explanation of how the method works,
- A description of the possible risks and side effects, including all major life-threatening risks and all common minor risks,
- A description of the benefits you can expect,
- An explanation of the alternative methods of birth control, including sterilization procedures
- An offer to answer any questions about the method that you might have,
- A reminder that you are free to change your mind at any time and that your decision to use the method is completely voluntary,
- A written document of informed consent—stating that you have received the above information—which you must sign.

PUTTING IT ALL TOGETHER

We've talked about five important areas to consider when you choose a method:

EFFECTIVENESS: will it protect me?

SAFETY: will it be safe for me?

FEELINGS AND LIFE-STYLE: do I understand what it would be like to use it?

REPRODUCTIVE LIFE PLAN: does it fit into my overall life goals?

INFORMED CONSENT: do I understand what I have a right and a responsibility to learn about?

It should be pretty clear to you by now that there is no *best* method. The best method *for you* is the one you and your partner feel best about using. So don't feel you *have to* use what your friends are using, because your needs can be very different from theirs.

And please remember that you can change your mind! If your first choice turns out to be a method you don't like after all, try another. Keep trying until you find a method that suits your needs. Also, remember that a year from now, or five years from now, you may want a different method. Needs change over time...for everybody.

After you read about the method you use or want to use, why not come back and read this chapter again? Make the best possible decision for yourself. *IT'S YOUR CHOICE.*

CHAPTER 2:
MENSTRUATION AND THE
CYCLE OF FERTILITY

THE MENSTRUAL CYCLE

Once boys reach puberty they become fertile. A fertile male is capable of fathering children. Men are fertile every day of the month. Once girls reach puberty they become fertile too. Women, however, are only fertile about once a month. A woman's egg lives about 24 to 48 hours after it is released from her ovary. Counting the overall time that sperm and an egg can remain active, a woman has about 7 fertile days each month: including the three days before and the three days after her ovulation day.

The length of a woman's fertility cycle is about four weeks. Each woman has approximately 300-400 fertile cycles in her lifetime, depending on the number of pregnancies she has, whether or not she breast-feeds, whether she uses birth control Pills, and the age she starts and stops having periods. Basically, an average 28-day cycle works like this:

Day 1: *Menstruation begins:* The lining of the uterus is shed because it does not have hormone support to keep it in place.

Day 2: *Menstruation continues:* The *hypothalamus*, at the base of the brain, notices there is very little hormone activity and sends a message to the nearby *pituitary gland.* The pituitary gland gets the message to start a cycle; it then puts out a hormone called FSH (follicle stimulating hormone). FSH is a signal for the ovary to start ripening an egg for release. Meanwhile, the ovary itself releases a hormone called ESTROGEN. Estrogen is a signal for the uterus to begin building up a new inner lining. The inner lining is preparing for pregnancy.

Day 14: *Ovary releases an egg.* Before the ovary can release an egg it has to get another hormone signal from the pituitary. The pituitary sends a hormone called LH (luteinizing hormone), which signals the ovary to release an egg. Also, LH tells the empty egg container, called a *follicle,* to turn itself into a hormone-producing gland on the ovary called a *corpus luteum.* The corpus luteum makes a hormone called PROGESTERONE—another signal to the uterus to further prepare its inner lining for pregnancy.

19

Day 26-28: *A pre-menstrual time occurs.* Levels of estrogen and progesterone drop to lower levels. Many women can tell they are about to have their period.

Day 1: *Menstruation begins.* The cycle has begun again!

You may be thinking, "How can all that be happening inside my body and I don't even know it?" This complex hormone cycle does have some signals that you can notice:

cramps—abdominal pains
lower back pain
leg pain
diarrhea
anxiety or irritability
depression
headaches
change in sex drive (increase or decrease)
acne

Around the time of ovulation
spotting or light bleeding
increased sex drive
pain, low in abdomen, on one side or the other
increase in normal discharge; discharge becomes clear and slippery

Days just before menstruation begins
weight gain
breast tenderness or fullness
anxiety
depression
headaches
bloated feeling due to fluid retention
acne
constipation

If you tune into your own cycle and keep a record on a calendar you may notice your own cycle signals.

1. You can learn what your cycles are like. If they change, you will notice it.
2. You can use the information to help you avoid pregnancy (see Chapter 9).
3. You can use the information to help you plan a pregnancy when you want to become pregnant.

THE MENSTRUAL CYCLE

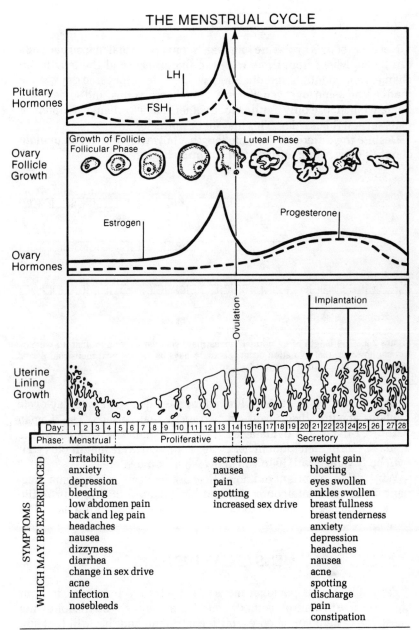

Figure 2:1 The menstrual cycle and symptoms which are associated with the different phases of the cycle.

CYCLE LENGTH

Not everybody's cycles are four weeks long. A normal menstrual cycle can be anywhere from three weeks to five weeks, and the length can change from month to month. Some women bleed for three days, some for five, and some for seven. Some women have cramps, and some don't. Some women lose only a little blood; others have to change tampons or pads several times a day. This may all be normal.

Despite the difference in cycle lengths, however, *all women ovulate about 14 days before the next menstruation begins.*

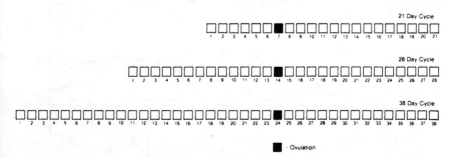

Figure 2:2 The length of a "normal" menstrual cycle varies from woman to woman. Notice, however, that ovulation occurs about 14 days before the next menstrual period regardless of the length of the cycle.

As you can see from this illustration, a woman with a 28-day cycle ovulates about *halfway between* two menstrual periods. The woman with a 21-day cycle ovulates *early* in her cycle. The woman with a 38-day cycle ovulates *late* in her cycle. Your own cycle length plus your own body signals will help you know when you ovulate.

Why is this important to know? Because you can only become pregnant if you have intercourse without birth control during your fertile week, which begins about 3 days before ovulation and ends 3 days after ovulation.

MENSTRUAL HISTORY

Facts about your personal menstrual cycles are important in your choice of a birth control method. Your doctor may ask you the following questions to help you choose a birth control method that will best suit you.

How old were you when you first started having menstrual periods?

When was your last menstrual period?

Have you missed any periods?

Does your cycle vary in length from month to month (21 days, then 28 days, etc.)?

Do you have cramping with your periods? If so, do the cramps interfere with your daily activities?

Do your periods usually last more than seven days? Do you soak more than five pads or tampons per day?

Do you ever have bleeding between periods?

Do you often have abdominal pain about halfway between two periods?

Do you notice depression, headaches, anxiety, weight gain, ankle swelling, breast tenderness or fullness just before you get your period?

Have your menstrual cycles been affected by your present birth control method (less bleeding, more cramps, etc.)?

Are there times during your cycle when you especially enjoy intercourse—or feel especially disinterested in sex.

COMMON QUESTIONS ABOUT MENSTRUATION

Can you become pregnant when you have intercourse during your menstrual period? Yes, you can. Although it is not common, it certainly has happened. It is most likely to happen to a woman who has short menstrual cycles (18-25 days).

Can you get pregnant if you have never had a period? Yes, you can. A young woman can ovulate and become pregnant a couple of weeks before she would have had her first period. Until a woman has definitely gone through menopause, or until she or her partner is sterilized, every act of intercourse in the fertile years should include a method of birth control if a couple does not want to reproduce.

Can you go swimming when you are having your period? You certainly can, and many women do. Sometimes this is tricky on the first day if bleeding is heavy or if cramps are extremely painful. Swimming or any type of vigorous exercise will help reduce cramping. Tampons should prevent most problems associated with heavy bleeding.

Are you unclean when you are having your period? NO!

Do you have to have menstrual periods before a doctor will let you have the Pill? Generally, yes...but not always. Most clinicians feel that it is important to wait until you have fairly regular periods before starting the Pill. This policy might help protect you from having trouble becom-

23

ing pregnant later when you are ready. Medical researchers are working to learn more about this subject.

TOXIC SHOCK SYNDROME

Toxic Shock Syndrome is a rare but serious illness that causes fever, muscle aches, severe diarrhea, fatigue, skin rash, and weakness. These symptoms in some cases progress rapidly, and can lead to low blood pressure, shock and even death. Most cases of toxic shock syndrome have occured in women, and have begun during a menstrual period when the woman was using tampons.

Researchers believe that toxic shock syndrome is caused by a toxin produced by Staphylococcus bacteria. Tampons appear to play a role in promoting bacterial growth or possibly in absorption of the toxin in the woman's body.

The link between toxic shock and tampons is not fully understood. Tampons have been used for many years, but toxic shock is a new problem. It may be that new "super absorbant" tampon products introduced in the last few years play a special role. Toxic shock has been reported with all the tampon brands available, and with natural sea sponges as well, but the super absorbant products can cause excessive drying of the vaginal tissue, and even vaginal ulcers. Damage to the vagina may explain why the bacterial growth thrives or why toxin is more readily absorbed.

A woman who stops using tampons can reduce her risk for toxic shock close to zero. Even among tampon-users, however, the risk is small. Out of 100,000 women, only about 3 would require hospital treatment for toxic shock each year. When toxic shock was first studied, about 10% of cases were fatal. Deaths have decreased now that women and their physicians are aware of the early danger signs of toxic shock. A woman who has toxic shock once has a much greater risk of recurrence during future menstrual periods if she continues to use tampons. Probably she continues to carry the bacteria.

Unfortunately, a woman may carry Staphylococcus bacteria in or around her vagina with no symptoms at all to warn her until menstrual blood and a tampon provides the chance for rapid bacterial growth and toxin release. Staphylococcus is a common skin bacteria, and also may be present in minor skin infections such as pimples or on herpes ulcers.

Common sense precautions may reduce your toxic shock risks:

1. Wash your hands carefully before inserting a tampon to minimize the chance of spreading staphylococcus bacteria from your fingers

to the tampon. Be particularly careful if you have any skin infection or herpes ulcers.

2. Change your tampon regularly—at least once every 8 hours or so.
3. Use tampons intermittently so that your vagina has "free time" each day; for example, use tampons during the day and pads at night.
4. Use tampons made of cotton or rayon; avoid tampons with new "super absorbant" fibers.
5. Don't use tampons for more than a few days at a time (5–7 days), and don't use tampsons when flow is light or your vagina feels dry.
6. If you have had toxic shock, or think you *may have had it*, don't use tampons until your clinician treats you and checks to be sure you are no longer carrying Staphylococcus bacteria.
7. Remember the toxic shock danger signs and watch carefully for them during your period. Early signs may be like flu, but be sure to see your clinician right away and stop using tampons in the meantime.
8. Toxic Shock Danger signs:

   ● FEVER (101°F or more)
   ● DIARRHEA
   ● MUSCLE ACHES
   ● FATIGUE AND WEAKNESS
   ● RASH

PAINFUL MENSTRUATION CRAMPS

Menstrual pain is the most common cause of discomfort during a woman's cycle. Indeed, cramps are one of the most common causes of young women missing school and older women missing work.

There are several different types of menstrual pain. One type occurs just before bleeding begins. At this time, a woman may feel heavy or bloated and have a dull aching pain in her lower abdomen. This type of pain is quite different from the sharp cramping pains some women have during their periods.

Cramping pain is caused by strong contractions of the uterus as it works to get rid of its inner lining. Cramps may also be caused by infections, an IUD, or a number of other factors. It may be that a good deal of the pain associated with menstruation and infection is related to the action of a powerful chemical the body produces called *prostaglandins*, which cause the uterus to contract and cramp.

25

Listed below are some home remedies that may be helpful for relief of menstrual pain:

- heating pad (on "low" to avoid burning skin)
- hot bath, sauna, or steam bath
- vigorous physical exercise such as running or swimming
- lower back, leg, or calf massage
- lying on side or back with knees to chest
- orgasm from sexual intercourse or masturbation
- an alcoholic beverage (wine, hot toddy, blackberry brandy, etc.)
- hot drinks (milk, tea, etc.... Some claim tamari and raspberry leaf teas have special benefits.)
- aspirin
- rest

If pain is severe or continues throughout your period, talk to your doctor. Here are some of the medical treatments which may be suggested.

- analgesics or narcotics (pain relievers that are stronger than aspirin)
- diuretics (help to get rid of extra body fluid)
- birth control Pills
- prostaglandin inhibitors
- insertion of an IUD which gives off progesterone
- dilation and curettage (D & C)

Lack of exercise, poor posture, and constipation can make menstrual cramps worse. Feeling worried or upset can cause muscle tension, which produces cramps as well. But, "An ounce of prevention is worth a pound of cure." Here's how:

Get plenty of rest
Eat a balanced diet
Exercise regularly
Eat less salt

BIRTH CONTROL AND MENSTRUATION

Certain birth control methods can influence menstrual pain dramatically. The combined birth control Pill and the Mini-Pill may relieve cramping because they often prevent ovulation. Pills may also decrease the amount and duration of menstrual bleeding, the severity of premenstrual fluid retention and pre-menstrual depression, the pain associated with ovulation, the amount of spotting, and flareups of acne during the menstrual cycle. (But, Pills can also make these same symptons worse.)

The IUD that contains progesterone, the Progestasert-T, can also decrease menstrual pain. Most IUDs, however, are more likely to increase menstrual cramps and bleeding. Cramps may also be increased by rim pressure from a diaphragm. Other methods, such as condoms, diaphragms, foam, suppositories, withdrawal, or fertility awareness have no effect on menstrual pain or bleeding.

MENOPAUSE

Usually betweeen the ages of 45 and 55 a woman experiences a change in her menstrual cycle. This change, often called the climacteric, menopause or "change of life", marks the end of a woman's ability to become pregnant and produce children.

As a woman ages, particularly in her mid-forties, her fertility declines. Over time the ovaries stop maturing eggs and producing estrogen until they do not respond to any hormones at all. The woman's menstrual periods become irregular and are less heavy; eventually they stop completely. This is called menopause.

Women experience different side effects during this period of their lives. Some women have no symptoms whatsoever or relatively few. Others may have hot flashes ("the sweats"), vaginal drying, changes in their menstrual patterns (lighter periods, fewer days of bleeding and skipped months), insomnia (lack of sleep), rapid beating of the heart and aches in the back, muscles and joints. Emotional symptoms may include nervousness, depression, tension, hopelessness and irritability.

If you are going through menopause you may notice some or all of these symptoms. **DO NOT BE ALARMED.** They are all normal. You may want to see your clinician for a gynecologic examination. Be sure you talk about the menopause and its side effects. In addition, you probably do not need to use birth control any longer if you have not had a period for about a year. This too should be discussed with your doctor.

Your clinician may recommend temporary treatment with estrogen hormones (estrogen replacement therapy or ERT) in order to ease your discomfort if you are suffering from vaginal dryness or hot flashes. Be sure you discuss the risks and benefits of this treatment before you begin taking hormones.

Remember, it is extremely important for you to continue to have your yearly gynecologic examination and tests (this should include a Pap smear). Continue to examine your breasts regularly. If you experience any bleeding or spotting after you have gone through menopause, see your doctor promptly.

CHAPTER 3: BIRTH CONTROL PILLS

The oral contraceptive Pill, if taken correctly, is very safe and very effective for most women. This chapter gives instructions to help you take the Pill correctly and help you decide if the Pill is a safe choice for you. The many advantages of the Pill are not discussed in this chapter. Read Chapter 1 to learn about the advantages and disadvantages of the Pill and to see how it compares with other birth control methods.

BEFORE YOU BEGIN TAKING PILLS, think about the following questions. If you have any YES answers be sure to discuss them with your clinician before you start Pills.

YES/NO 1. Is there a chance I might be pregnant right now?

YES/NO 2. Is there any chance I may have liver damage because of mononucleosis, hepatitis, alcoholism, or a liver tumor from the past?

YES/NO 3. Am I having abnormal vaginal bleeding now?

YES/NO 4. Have I ever had any of the following medical problems?
Blood clotting disorders such as thrombophlebitis (clots in leg vein or elsewhere) or pulmonary embolism (clots in the lung)
Heart attack or stroke
Cancer (including skin cancer)
High blood pressure (including high blood pressure or toxemia of pregnancy)
Diabetes
Gall bladder disease
Yellow jaundice (including jaundice of pregnancy)
Sickle cell disease
Fibrocystic breast disease
Pap smear that was precancerous (dysplasia, CIN, Class 3 or 4)
Migraine headaches
Heart disease or kidney disease
Epilepsy
Asthma
Varicose veins

Severe acne

Fibroid tumors of the uterus

Very irregular menstrual periods (long delays)

Suicide attempt or serious depression

YES/NO   5. Has anyone in my family had diabetes or breast cancer?

YES/NO   6. Do I anticipate major surgery within the next month?

YES/NO   7. Do I have a serious leg injury or a cast on my leg?

YES/NO   8. Am I a heavy smoker (15 cigarettes a day or more)?

YES/NO   9. Have I just recently started having menstrual periods?

YES/NO   10. Am I over 35 years old?

YES/NO   11. Am I a DES (diethylstilbestrol) daughter?

YES/NO   12. Am I breast-feeding now?

YES/NO   13. Have I completed a full-term pregnancy within the last 2 weeks?

YES/NO   14. Am I taking any drugs or medications?

YES/NO   15. Have I had problems with Pills in the past such as high blood pressure, weight gain, headaches, hair loss, darkened patches on my face, or depression?

YES/NO   16. Will I have any difficulty getting back to see my clinician if a problem occurs?

IMPORTANT THINGS TO REMEMBER

1. **REMEMBER THE PILL DANGER SIGNS.** If you develop any of these signs you **MUST** see your clinician right away. They are the warnings of serious—even deadly—Pill complications.

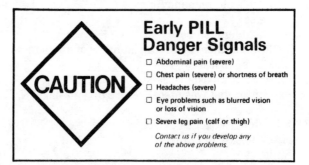

Figure 3:1   These signals are alerting you to a possible medical complication. Contact your clinician immediately if you notice any of these symptoms.

2. **IF YOU HAVE ANY SERIOUS MEDICAL PROBLEMS** be sure the clinician who treats you knows that you are taking Pills, even if the problem seems completely unrelated to birth control. Also, any time you have a new medical problem, remember to check the list of questions at the beginning of this chapter. You may need to talk with your clinician to see whether Pills are still a reasonable choice for you.

COMMON CAUSES OF ACCIDENTAL PREGNANCY

1. **RUNNING OUT OF PILLS** and not getting a refill in time to stay on schedule. Even one week of delay is often enough to allow ovulation to occur and make pregnancy likely. This is an especially sad cause of accidental pregnancy because in most circumstances your clinician can authorize an emergency one-month refill by phone to a drugstore.

2. **STOPPING PILLS** because of a problem and not getting started with another birth control method soon enough. When you stop taking Pills, you can expect to ovulate within 2 weeks. That means you are fertile soon after your last Pill.

3. **MISSING TWO OR MORE PILLS** in one cycle. Forgetting to take Pills along on a weekend trip is especially common.

STARTING PILLS

Begin your first package of Pills any time within the first 7 days of a normal menstrual cycle. (Day 1 is the first day of bleeding with a normal period.) This lets you know that you are not pregnant when you begin Pills, and means there is a good chance that you will not ovulate even in your very first Pill cycle. Do use a backup method such as condoms, foam, or diaphragm for the first two weeks that you take Pills.

For example, if your menstrual period starts on Wednesday you can begin taking Pills the very next day, or any day in the next week (up to Tuesday). Use your backup method until you have finished 14 Pills.

Your Pill schedule is quite simple; you will take one Pill each day for three weeks (21 days) and then have one week with no Pill, or with blank Pills (placebos) that contain no hormones. You will have your menstrual period during your week off Pills. Three weeks on Pills, one week off. Many clinicians recommend the *Start on Sunday* plan because it is easy to remember and, for most women, means that menstrual periods will not occur on weekends.

⊠ = Pill Day

The 21-day pill schedule using the
Start-on-Sunday Method

⊠ = Pill Day

Using the 28-day pill schedule, there
are no days without pills.

Usually a
different
color pill

Figure 3:2   Starting regular birth control pills.

You are fully protected against pregnancy after you have taken your
very first 14 Pills, as long as you stick to your Pill schedule. You are
protected on the 21 days you take Pills and on the 7 days off Pills (or the 7
blank Pill days). If you delay starting a new Pill pack and have more than
7 days without Pills, chances are good you will ovulate, and that can
mean pregnancy. Be especially sure to start each new pack promptly so
you have only 7 days—no more—off Pills.

INSTRUCTIONS FOR USING PILLS

1. **HAVE A BACKUP BIRTH CONTROL METHOD** on hand such as foam, condoms, spermicidal tablets or suppositories, or a diaphragm. You will
need to **USE YOUR BACKUP METHOD:**
  ● while you are waiting to start Pills,
  ● during your very first 14 days while on Pills, and
  ● later on if you miss Pills or stop taking them for any reason.
2. **SWALLOW 1 PILL EACH DAY** until you finish your Pill pack. If you are
using a 21-day pack, stop taking Pills for 1 week, then start your new
pack. If you are using a 28-day pack, begin a new pack immediately. The
last 7 Pills in a 28-day pack are *blank* tablets (placebos) that contain no
hormones. When you take these last 7 Pills, consider this your week off
Pills.
3. **IF YOU MISS 1 PILL** take it (yesterday's Pill) as soon as you remember.
Take today's Pill at the regular time, even if that means you take 2 Pills in
one day. If you miss only 1 Pill, pregnancy is not likely, but you could
use your backup birth control method until you finish the rest of the Pills
in that pack, to be extra careful.

4. IF YOU MISS 2 PILLS IN A ROW take 2 Pills as soon as you remember and 2 Pills the next day. Then go back to taking 1 Pill each day. **BE SURE TO USE YOUR BACKUP METHOD OF BIRTH CONTROL** until you have finished that pack of Pills.

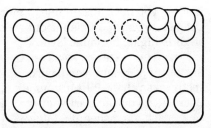

21-Day Combined Birth Control Pill Package

Two Pills missed. Extra Pill taken for next 2 days. Use of backup contraceptive advised for rest of that cycle (until next menstrual period starts).

5. IF YOU MISS 3 OR MORE PILLS IN A ROW there is a good chance you will ovulate and become pregnant. Immediately start using your backup method. You will need to start a whole new Pill schedule from the beginning. Wait until a menstrual period starts. (Chances are good that you will already be bleeding or will bleed soon after missing that many Pills.) Begin a new pack of Pills any time within the first seven days of bleeding. For example, if bleeding starts on Friday, you could take your first Pill from a new pack the following Sunday. Continue using your backup method until you have taken 14 Pills from the new pack. If your menstrual period does not begin within 4 to 6 weeks, see your clinician for an exam and pregnancy test.

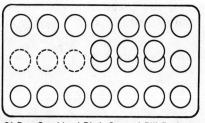

21-Day Combined Birth Control Pill Package

Three Pills missed. Extra Pills taken for next 3 days. Use of back-up contraceptive strongly recommended for rest of that cycle (until next menstrual starts).

ALTERNATIVE METHOD OF
BIRTH CONTROL MIGHT BE
BETTER THAN PILLS
FOR PATIENT
WHO MISSES 3 IN A ROW!!

6. IF YOU HAVE SPOTTING OR BLEEDING during your 21 active Pill days, keep on taking your Pills on schedule anyway. **IF YOUR BLEEDING IS VERY HEAVY OR IF YOU HAVE CRAMPS, PAIN, OR FEVER, SEE YOUR CLINICIAN RIGHT AWAY.** Your bleeding may be caused by infection. In most cases bleeding is not serious and will often stop after a few days. Bleeding is especially likely if you have missed one or more Pills. If the bleeding persists you can talk to your clinician about switching to another Pill brand with a slightly higher hormone level.

7. **IF YOU SKIP A MENSTRUAL PERIOD**, and are sure you have correctly taken all the Pills in your last pack, then you can start your next new pack on schedule (after 7 days) anyway. If you think you may have missed Pills in your last pack or you have missed 2 periods in a row, you should arrange to see your clinician. In the meantime, use your backup method and **DO NOT** take Pills. You need to have an exam and pregnancy test before your return to Pills.

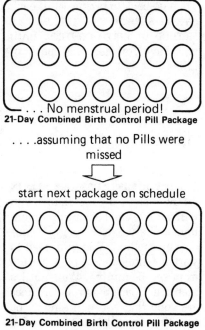

. . . No menstrual period!

21-Day Combined Birth Control Pill Package

. . . .assuming that no Pills were missed

start next package on schedule

21-Day Combined Birth Control Pill Package

Restart taking Pill on the same schedule even though period has not occurred.

8. **IF YOU BECOME ILL**, with severe diarrhea lasting more than one day, or if you are treated with antibiotics for any reason, then you may want to use your backup method of birth control while you finish that Pill pack. This will give you extra protection in case your illness or the medication you take interferes with the Pill's effectiveness.

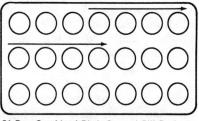

21-Day Combined Birth Control Pill Package

Diarrhea for 8 Days. Use of backup contraceptive advised for rest of that cycle (until next menstrual period starts).

34

9. **IF YOU DECIDE YOU WANT TO BECOME PREGNANT,** plan to stop using Pills and change to another method of birth control, such as condoms, for at least 2 or 3 months. Once off Pills, your natural cycle will be reestablished. Your clinician will be able to determine your pregnancy due-date more accurately if you have at least 2 natural menstrual periods before you become pregnant.

10. **SEE YOU CLINICIAN REGULARLY FOR ROUTINE CHECKUPS,** at least once a year. Be sure to have your blood pressure checked along with a Pap smear, breast exam, and pelvic exam.

STOPPING PILLS

You can stop Pills any time you want to, even in the middle of a Pill pack. Remember, though, that *protection from the birth control pill does not last after you stop.* Begin using another method the very next day after your last Pill. When you stop, you will probably have bleeding within 2 or 3 days after your last Pill. This is your final *Pill period.* After that, your body will reestablish its own natural cycle. You can expect your first menstrual period in about 4 to 6 weeks.

PROBLEMS TO WATCH·FOR

THE PILL DANGER SIGNS. Being alert to the danger signs can save your life. For most women the likelihood of having a serious problem is *rare.* Your clinician will help you decide if the Pill is a safe choice for you. For more perspective on the risks of having a serious problem from the Pill, see page 7 in Chapter 1. You can remember the Pill danger signs by thinking of the word **ACHES.**

A: **ABDOMINAL PAIN**—can mean gall bladder disease, ectopic (tubal) pregnancy, liver tumor, a blood clot or pancreas inflammation.

C: **CHEST PAIN OR SHORTNESS OF BREATH**—can mean blood clots in the lung or a heart attack.

H: **HEADACHES**—severe headaches may give advance warning of a stroke or dangerously high blood pressure.

E: **EYE PROBLEMS**—blurred vision, double vision, flashing lights, or partial blindness can mean stroke, high blood pressure, or clots in the eye blood vessels.

S: **SEVERE LEG PAIN**—persistent pain in the calf or thigh can mean blood clots in the leg.

If you have any of these problems, STOP TAKING PILLS AND SEE YOUR CLINI-CIAN RIGHT AWAY, even if you are not sure whether the problem is serious. If you can't get in touch with your clinician, then go to any hospital emergency room. Meanwhile, remember to use your backup method of birth control.

In addition to the immediate emergency danger signs above, you should watch for the following signs of possible medical problems with Pills:

1. BREAST LUMPS—While you are taking Pills you are less likely to develop a breast cyst than you would be normally. If you do find a lump or cyst, however, be sure to see your clinician.

2. YELLOW JAUNDICE—Liver problems can cause your skin and eyes to have a yellow tint. See your clinician. You may be having a Pill complication, or you may have hepatitis or mononucleosis. In any case you will need to stop taking Pills and change to another method.

3. SEVERE DEPRESSION—If you are having problems with depression or thinking about suicide, see your clinician right away. Pills can cause or aggravate depression. Your clinician may recommend Vitamin B6 (50 milligrams a day) or may suggest you use another method of birth control.

4. A NEW MOLE OR A MOLE THAT IS CHANGING OR GROWING—A rare type of skin cancer called malignant melanoma may be linked to Pill use. If you have a suspicious mole, be sure to discuss it with your clinician.

5. BREAST MILK—Pills sometimes cause breast milk production. Be sure to see your clinician if this occurs. Breast milk may indicate problems unrelated to Pills.

The following problems related to Pill use are less serious medically, but are more common to Pill users:

6. SHORT AND LIGHT MENSTRUAL PERIODS—Your periods are likely to become shorter and lighter when you take Pills. As long as you have at least a little bleeding each cycle this is not really a problem. If your periods disappear completely, however, talk to your clinician. You may need to change to a slightly higher hormone brand, because if you don't have any bleeding, it is hard to be sure you are not pregnant each cycle.

7. SPOTTING OR BLEEDING BETWEEN PERIODS—Don't be alarmed if you have this problem, especially the first month or two that you take Pills. Keep taking your Pills on schedule. Your clinician may call it break-through bleeding and may recommend a change in Pill brands if it continues. If you are taking other medications, such as antibiotics, when breakthrough bleeding occurs, talk to your clinician. It may be a good

idea for you to use your backup birth control method until you finish your current Pill pack.

8. NAUSEA—Very few women have nausea with the low dose Pills most often prescribed. Even if you do have this problem, the feeling of nausea will probably stop after your first few Pill days. Try taking your Pill at bedtime or dinner time to decrease the nausea. Talk to your clinician if the problem persists.

9. WEIGHT GAIN—Weight gain is not common with the low dose Pills used today. If you find that you are having problems with weight, talk to your clinician. A change in Pill brand may help, or you may need to switch to another method of birth control. Pills definitely CAN cause weight gain.

10. CHANGE IN ACNE—Your acne may improve while you are taking Pills, or it may become worse. If you are having problems, talk to your clinician. A change in Pill brands may help.

11. DARK PATCHES ON YOUR FACE (chloasma)—Some Pill users develop dark skin areas on the upper lip, checks, and forehead, similar to *pregnancy rash*. It usually fades when you stop taking Pills. Avoid sun exposure or use a sun screen to reduce this problem.

12. HAIR CHANGES—Loss of hair (on the head) or an increase in hair growth on the body and face can be caused by Pills. A change in Pill brand is sometimes helpful.

13. VAGINAL YEAST INFECTIONS—Pills make yeast infections more likely. Yeast treatment is usually effective, even while you continue taking Pills.

14. MOOD CHANGES—You may notice depression, irritability, or a change in sex drive. If your moods are severe, be sure to talk to your clinician.

TIPS FOR SUCCESS

1. MEMORIZE THE PILL DANGER SIGNS. See your clinician IMMEDIATELY even if your symptoms are not severe.

2. DO WHAT YOU CAN TO REDUCE YOUR PILL RISKS.
- Cut down or stop smoking.
- Stop taking Pills if you have a Pill-related medical problem.
- Stick with low dosage Pills: 50 micrograms of estrogen or less.
- Be faithful about routine checkups.
- If you are over 30, think about switching to another method of birth control. Don't think of Pills as a permanent solution to your birth

control needs. Some Pill risks increase the longer you take Pills; 5 years is a good time to begin thinking of other options.

• Be sure to tell any clinician taking care of you *for any problem* that you are taking birth control Pills.

3. **FIND A COMFORTABLE ROUTINE FOR REMEMBERING YOUR PILL.** Take your Pill at about the same time every day; pick the best time for you. Use any trick you need to remember: tape a sign on your bathroom mirror, keep your Pill pack next to the orange juice.

4. **CHECK YOUR PACK EACH MORNING OR NIGHT** to be sure that you did take your last Pill on schedule.

5. **MAKE A DOCTOR'S APPOINTMENT** so you can get your Pills refilled in plenty of time. When you start your last Pill pack, be sure you will have your new supply on time. If an emergency arises (your Pills were lost in the apartment trash compactor), call your clinician. Usually, a temporary refill can be arranged by telephone.

6. **IF YOU WANT TO CHANGE YOUR PILL SCHEDULE,** call your clinician. You can change the timing of your cycle if you want to avoid a period during vacation, for example. Your clinician can help you calculate the changes so that your birth control protection will not be altered.

GO BACK TO YOUR CLINICIAN

1. **IF YOU HAVE A PILL DANGER SIGN:**
   A: Abdominal pain
   C: Chest pain, shortness of breath
   H: Headaches (severe)
   E: Eye problems
   S: Severe leg pain

2. **IF YOU HAVE A BREAST LUMP, YELLOW JAUNDICE, SEVERE DEPRESSION, A NEW MOLE, OR BREAST MILK.**

3. **IF YOU MISS TWO PERIODS IN A ROW** (or one period when you think, for any reason, that you might be pregnant).

4. **IF YOU HAVE PILL SIDE EFFECTS OR PROBLEMS.**

5. **WHEN YOU NEED YOUR PILLS REFILLED.**

6. **FOR ROUTINE VISITS** every 6 to 12 months for a blood pressure check, Pap smear, breast exam, abdominal exam, and pelvic exam.

CHAPTER 4: MINI-PILLS (PROGESTIN-ONLY PILLS)

Even though Mini-Pills are not the same as regular combined birth control Pills, the questions you need to think about are the same. Because there have as yet been no large, long-term studies to show how complication rates for Mini-Pill users differ from complication rates for women who use combined birth control Pills, the safest approach is to consider the same problems for both. Read Chapter 1 to learn more about the Mini-Pill and its many advantages, and to see how it compares with combined Pills.

Mini-Pills contain a progestin only—no estrogen. Combined birth control Pills contain both progestin and estrogen. Compared with the amount of progestin in combined birth control Pills, the amount of progestin in each Mini-Pill is quite low. Many clinicians feel, therefore, that risks with Mini-Pills should be lower than risks with combined Pills. However, some risks are linked to progestins. The starred (**) questions below are especially important for Mini-Pill users because these problems may be caused by progestin.

BEFORE YOU BEGIN TAKING MINI-PILLS, think about the following questions. If you have any **YES** answers be sure to discuss them with your clinician.

YES/NO 1. Is there a chance I might be pregnant right now?

YES/NO 2. Is there any chance I may have liver damage because of mononucleosis, hepatitis, alcoholism or a liver tumor in the past?

YES/NO 3. Am I having abnormal vaginal bleeding now?

YES/NO 4. Have I ever had any of the following medical problems?
Blood clotting disorders, such as thrombophlebitis (clots in leg vein or elsewhere) or pulmonary embolism (clots in the lung)
Heart attack or stroke
Cancer (including skin cancer)
High blood pressure (including high blood pressure or toxemia of pregnancy)
Diabetes**
Gallbladder disease**

Yellow jaundice (including jaundice of pregnancy)**
Sickle cell disease
Fibrocystic breast disease
Pap smear that was precancerous (dysplasia, CIN, Class 3 or 4)
Migraine headaches
Heart disease or kidney disease
Epilepsy**
Asthma
Varicose veins
Very irregular menstrual periods
Severe acne**
Fibroid tumors of the uterus
Suicide attempt or serious depression**

YES/NO 5. Has anyone in my family had diabetes or breast cancer?**
YES/NO 6. Do I have a serious leg injury or a cast on my leg?
YES/NO 7. Am I taking any drugs or medications?
YES/NO 8. Have I had in the past problems with Pills, such as high blood pressure, weight gain, headaches, hair loss, darkened patches on my face, depression?

IMPORTANT THINGS TO REMEMBER

1. REMEMBER THE PILL AND MINI-PILL DANGER SIGNS. If you develop any of these signs you MUST see your clinician right away. They are the warnings of serious—even deadly—pill complications.

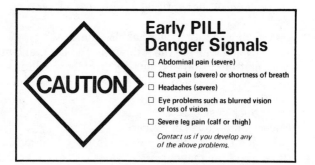

Figure 4:1 These signals are alerting you to a possible medical complication. Contact your clinician immediately if you notice any of these symptoms.

40

2. **IF YOU HAVE ANY SERIOUS MEDICAL PROBLEMS**, be sure the clinician who treats you knows that you are taking Mini-Pills, even if the problem seems completely unrelated to birth control Pills. Any time you have a new medical problem, remember to check the list of questions at the beginning of this chapter. You may need to talk with your clinician to see whether Mini-Pills are still a reasonable choice for you.

COMMON CAUSES OF ACCIDENTAL PREGNANCY

1. **RUNNING OUT OF PILLS**, not getting a refill in time to stay on schedule. Even a few days of delay is often enough to allow ovulation to occur and make pregnancy likely. This is an especially sad cause of accidental pregnancy because in most circumstances your clinician can authorize an emergency one-month refill by phone to a drugstore.

2. **STOPPING MINI-PILLS BECAUSE OF A PROBLEM**, and not starting another birth control method soon enough. When you stop Mini-Pills, you can expect to ovulate within a week or so. That means you are fertile soon after your last Pill.

3. **MISSING 1 OR MORE MINI-PILLS** in one cycle. Forgetting to take along Mini-Pills on a weekend trip is especially common.

STARTING PILLS

Begin your first package of Mini-Pills on the first day of a normal menstrual cycle. (Day 1 is the first day of bleeding with a normal period.) This lets you know that you are not pregnant when you begin Mini-Pills, and means there is a good chance that you will not ovulate even during your very first Mini-Pill cycle. Do use a backup method, such as condoms, foam, or diaphragm, for the first 2 weeks that you take Pills.

For example, if your menstrual period starts on Wednesday, begin taking the Mini-Pill the very same day (Wednesday). Use your backup method until you have finished 14 Pills.

Your Mini-Pill schedule is quite simple: You will take 1 Pill each day for as long as you want to use Mini-Pills. There are no *breaks* or *weeks off* when you take Mini-Pills. Take 1 Mini-Pill each day, even during your period. Your menstrual (period) cycle may be changed by Mini-Pills, or it may remain the same as it was before.

After you have taken your very first 14 Mini-Pills, you have full birth control protection continuously, as long as you take 1 Mini-Pill each day. If you delay starting a new Pill pack, or have more than 1 or 2 days without Mini-Pills, chances are that you will not be adequately protected. That can mean pregnancy. Be especially sure to start each new pack promptly so you have no interruption in hormones and little chance of pregnancy.

INSTRUCTIONS FOR USING MINI-PILLS

1. **HAVE A BACKUP BIRTH CONTROL METHOD** on hand such as foam, spermicidal tablets or suppositories, condoms, or a diaphragm. You will need to **USE YOUR BACKUP METHOD:**
   - while you are waiting to start Mini-Pills,
   - during your very first 14 days on Mini-Pills, and
   - later on if you miss 1 Mini-Pill or stop taking them for any reason.

2. **SWALLOW 1 PILL EACH DAY** until you finish your Pill pack. Then start your new pack the next day.

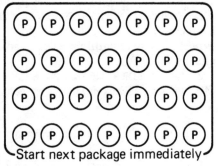

Progestin-Only Pill or Mini-Pill Package

Pills contain a progestin but no estrogen.

Start next package immediately

3. **IF YOU MISS 1 MINI-PILL,** take it (yesterday's Mini-Pill) as soon as you remember. Also take today's Mini-Pill at the regular time, even if that means 2 Pills in 1 day. For extra protection, you could use your backup birth control method until your next menstrual period starts.

4. **IF YOU MISS 2 MINI-PILLS IN A ROW,** take 2 Mini-Pills as soon as you remember and 2 Mini-Pills the next day. Then go back to taking 1 Mini-Pill each day. **BE SURE TO USE YOUR BACKUP METHOD OF BIRTH CONTROL** until you have your next menstrual period.

5. **IF YOU MISS 3 OR MORE MINI-PILLS** in a row, there is a good chance you could ovulate and become pregnant. **Immediately start using your backup method.** You should start a whole new Mini-Pill schedule from the beginning. Wait until a menstrual period starts. (Chances are good that you will bleed soon after missing that many Mini-Pills.) Begin a new pack of Mini-Pills on the first day of bleeding. Meanwhile, continue using your backup method until you have taken 14 Mini-Pills from the

42

new pack. If your menstrual period does not begin within 4 to 6 weeks, see your clinician for an exam and a pregnancy test.

6. **KEEP TRACK OF YOUR PERIODS** while you take Mini-Pills. If you have more than 45 days with no period, then stop taking Mini-Pills, and see your clinician for an exam and pregnancy test.

7. **IF YOU HAVE SPOTTING OR FREQUENT MENSTRUAL BLEEDING**, keep taking your Mini-Pills on schedule anyway. If your *bleeding is very heavy or if you have cramps, pain, or fever, see your clinician right away.* Your bleeding may be caused by infection. In most cases, bleeding is not serious and will often stop after a few days. Bleeding is especially likely if you have missed one or more Mini-Pills. Bleeding is common during the first few months a woman takes Mini-Pills, but if bleeding persists, you can talk to your clinician about switching to another Mini-Pill brand that provides a slightly higher hormone level.

8. **IF YOU BECOME ILL** with severe diarrhea, lasting more than one day, or if you are treated with antibiotics for any reason, then you may want to use your backup method of birth control along with your Mini-Pills until your next menstrual period. This will give you extra protection in case your illness or the medication interferes with Mini-Pill effectiveness.

9. **IF YOU DECIDE YOU WANT TO BECOME PREGNANT**, plan to stop using Mini-Pills and change to another method of birth control, such as condoms, for at least 2 or 3 months. Once off Mini-Pills, your natural cycle will soon be reestablished. Your clinician will be able to determine your pregnancy due–date more accurately if you have at least 2 natural menstrual periods before you become pregnant.

10. **SEE YOUR CLINICIAN REGULARLY** for routine checkups. At least once a year, be sure to have a blood pressure check, Pap smear, breast exam, and pelvic exam.

STOPPING MINI-PILLS

You can stop Mini-Pills any time you want to, even in the middle of a Mini-Pill pack. Remember, though, that *protection from the Mini-Pill does not last after your stop.* Begin using another method the very next day. When you stop, you will probably have bleeding within 2 or 3 days after your last Pill. After that, your body will reestablish its own natural cycle. You can expect your first menstrual period in about 4 to 6 weeks.

PROBLEMS TO WATCH FOR

THE MINI-PILL DANGER SIGNS. Being alert to the danger signs can save your life. For most women, the likelihood of having a serious problem is *rare*, probably more rare than may be had with combined Pills. Your clinician will help you decide if the Mini-Pill is a safe choice for you. For more perspective on the risks of having a serious problem from Mini-Pills, see page 8 in Chapter 1. You can remember the Pill danger signs by thinking of the word ACHES.

A: ABDOMINAL PAIN—can mean gall bladder disease, ectopic (tubal) pregnancy, liver tumor, a blood clot, or pancreas inflammation.

C: CHEST PAIN OR SHORTNESS OF BREATH—can mean blood clots in the lung or a heart attack.

H: HEADACHES—severe headaches may give advance warning of a stroke or dangerously high blood pressure.

E: EYE PROBLEMS—blurred vision, double vision, flashing lights, or partial blindness can mean stroke, high blood pressure, or clots in the eye blood vessels.

S: SEVERE LEG PAIN—Persistent pain in the calf or thigh can mean blood clots in the leg.

If you have any of these problems, STOP TAKING MINI-PILLS AND SEE YOUR CLINICIAN RIGHT AWAY, even if you are not sure whether the problem is serious. If you can't get in touch with your clinician, then go to any hospital emergency room. Meanwhile, remember to use your backup method of birth control.

In addition to the immediate emergency danger signs above, you should watch for the following signs of possible medical problems with Mini-Pills:

1. BREAST LUMPS—If you do find a lump or cyst, be sure to see your clinician.

2. YELLOW JAUNDICE—Liver problems can cause your skin and eyes to have a yellow tint. See you clinician. You may be having a Mini-Pill complication, or you may have hepatitis or mononucleosis. In any case, you will need to stop Mini-Pills and change to another method.

3. SEVERE DEPRESSION—If you are having problems with depression or thinking about suicide, see your clinician right away. Mini-Pills can cause or aggravate depression. Your clinician may recommend Vitamin B6 (50 milligrams a day) or may suggest you use another method of birth control.

4. **A NEW MOLE OR A MOLE THAT IS CHANGING OR GROWING**—A rare type of skin cancer called malignant melanoma may be linked to Mini-Pill use. If you have a suspicious mole, be sure to discuss it with your clinician.

5. **BREAST MILK**—Mini-Pills sometimes trigger breast milk production. Be sure to see your clinician if this occurs. Breast milk may indicate problems unrelated to Mini-Pills.

The following problems related to use of the Mini-Pill are less serious medically, but are more common for Mini-Pill users:

6. **SHORT AND LIGHT MENSTRUAL PERIODS OR IRREGULAR PERIODS**—Your periods are likely to become less regular, shorter, and lighter when you take Mini-Pills. As long as you have at least a little bleeding every 45 days, this is not really a problem. If your periods disappear completely, however, talk to your clinician. You may need to change to a slightly higher hormone brand. If you don't have *any* bleeding, it is hard to be sure you are not pregnant.

7. **SPOTTING OR BLEEDING BETWEEN PERIODS**—Don't be alarmed if you have this problem, especially the first month or two that you take Mini-Pills. Keep taking your Mini-Pills. Your clinician may call it *breakthrough* bleeding and may recommend a change in Mini-Pill brand if it continues. If you are taking other medications, such as antibiotics, when breakthrough bleeding occurs, talk to your clinician. It may be a good idea for you to use your backup birth control method until your next menstrual period.

8. **NAUSEA**—Very few women have nausea with the Mini-Pills. If you do, the feeling of nausea will probably stop after your first few Mini-Pill days. Try taking your Mini-Pill at bedtime or dinner time to lessen the nausea. Talk to your clinician if the problem persists.

9. **WEIGHT GAIN**—Weight gain is not common with the low dose Mini-Pills used today. If you find that you are having problems with weight, talk to your clinician. A change in brand may help, or you may need to switch to another method of birth control.

10. **CHANGE IN ACNE**—Your acne may improve while you are taking Mini-Pills, or it may become worse. If you are having problems, talk to your clinician. A change in brand may help.

11. **DARK PATCHES ON YOUR FACE** (chloasma)—Some Mini-Pill users develop dark skin areas on the upper lip, cheeks and forehead, similar to *pregnancy rash*. It usually fades when you stop taking Mini-Pills. Avoid sun exposure or use a sun screen to reduce this problem.

12. **HAIR CHANGES**—Loss of hair (on the head) or an increase in hair growth on the body and face can be caused by Mini-Pills. A change in brand is sometimes helpful.

13. **VAGINAL YEAST INFECTIONS**—Mini-Pills make yeast infections more likely. Yeast treatment is usually effective, even while you continue taking Mini-Pills.

14. **MOOD CHANGES**—You may notice depression, irritability, or a change in sex drive. If your moods are severe, be sure to talk to your clinician.

TIPS FOR SUCCESS

1. **MEMORIZE THE PILL DANGER SIGNS.** See your clinician **IMMEDIATELY** even if your symptoms are not severe.

2. **DO WHAT YOU CAN TO REDUCE YOUR MINI-PILL RISKS.**
- Cut down or stop smoking!
- Stop Mini-Pills promptly if you have a Pill-related medical problem.
- Be faithful about routine checkups.
- If you are over 30, think about switching to another method of birth control. Don't think of Mini-Pills as a permanent solution to your birth control needs. Some Pill risks increase the longer you take Mini-Pills; 5 years is a good time to begin thinking of other options.
- Be sure to tell any clinician taking care of you *for any problem* that you are taking Mini-Pills.

3. **FIND A COMFORTABLE ROUTINE FOR REMEMBERING YOUR MINI-PILL.** Take your Mini-Pill at about the same time every day; pick the best time for you. Use any trick you need to remember: Tape a sign on your bathroom mirror, keep your Mini-Pill pack next to the orange juice.

4. **CHECK YOUR PILL PACK EACH MORNING OR NIGHT** to be sure that you did take your last Mini-Pill on schedule.

5. **MAKE A DOCTOR'S APPOINTMENT** so you can get your pills refilled in plenty of time. When you start your last Mini-Pill pack, be sure you will have your new supply on time. If an emergency arises (your Mini-Pills were lost in the apartment trash compactor), call your clinician. A temporary refill can usually be arranged by telephone.

GO BACK TO YOUR CLINICIAN

1. **IF YOU HAVE A PILL DANGER SIGN:**
   A: Abdominal pain
   C: Chest pain, shortness of breath
   H: Headaches (severe)
   E: Eye problems
   S: Severe leg pain

2. IF YOU HAVE A BREAST LUMP, YELLOW JAUNDICE, SEVERE DEPRESSION, A NEW MOLE, OR BREAST MILK.

3. IF IT HAS BEEN MORE THAN 45 DAYS SINCE YOUR LAST PERIOD, or you think for any reason that you might be pregnant.

4. IF YOU HAVE MINI-PILL SIDE EFFECTS OR PROBLEMS.

5. WHEN YOU NEED YOUR MINI-PILLS REFILLED.

6. FOR ROUTINE VISITS, every 6 to 12 months, to check your blood pressure, have a Pap smear, breast exam, abdominal exam, and pelvic exam.

CHAPTER 5:
INTRAUTERINE DEVICES
(IUDS)

The IUD can be a safe and effective method for many women. This chapter may help you decide if the IUD is a good choice for you. This chapter also teaches you about the side effects of the IUD. The advantages of the IUD (and there are many) are not discussed here; read Chapter 1 to learn more about the IUD and to see how it compares with other birth control methods.

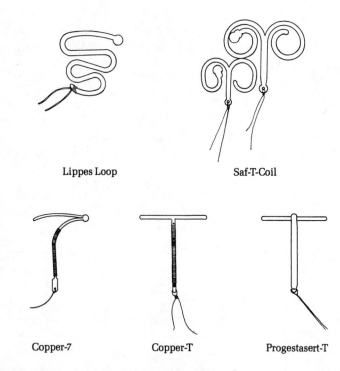

Lippes Loop   Saf-T-Coil

Copper-7   Copper-T   Progestasert-T

Figure 5:1 Five Food and Drug Administration approved IUDs which are available today in the United States.

BEFORE YOU HAVE AN IUD INSERTED, think about the following questions. If you have any YES answers, be sure to discuss them with your clinician.

YES/NO   1. Is there any chance I might be *pregnant* right now?

YES/NO   2. Is there a chance I might have *gonorrhea*? Do I have any signs of pelvic infection: pain in the lower abdomen, pain during intercourse, abnormal bleeding, or discharge?

YES/NO   3. Have I had a pelvic infection in the last two to six months, or repeated episodes of pelvic infection in the past?

YES/NO   4. Have I had an *ectopic (tubal) pregnancy* in the past?

YES/NO   5. Do I have any of the following medical problems?
>   Abnormal Pap smear results
>   Abnormal thickening of the uterine lining (hyperplasia)
>   Fibroids of the uterus
>   Polyps of the uterus
>   Abnormal uterus size or shape
>   Allergy to copper or jewelry
>   Diabetes
>   Rheumatic heart disease

YES/NO   6. Am I taking steroids (for asthma, arthritis, etc.) or anticoagulants (for blood-thinning)?

YES/NO   7. Do I have severe problems with menstrual cramps or a heavy blood flow?

YES/NO   8. Have I had gonorrhea in the past? Am I exposed to multiple sexual partners?

YES/NO   9. Do I want to become pregnant sometime in the future?

YES/NO 10. Will I have any difficulty seeing or calling my clinician for help if I have problems with an IUD?

YES/NO 11. Have I in the past had problems with passing out or fainting (for example, while at the dentist or when having a blood test).

IMPORTANT THINGS TO REMEMBER

1. MAKE YOUR HEALTH YOUR FIRST PRIORITY. If you have symptoms found on the danger sign list, see your clinician or go to an emergency room immediately. Often, early danger signs are mild, but *early* is the best time for treatment and cure. So put your job or school second—and your health first.

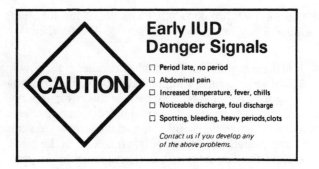

Early IUD Danger Signals

☐ Period late, no period
☐ Abdominal pain
☐ Increased temperature, fever, chills
☐ Noticeable discharge, foul discharge
☐ Spotting, bleeding, heavy periods, clots

Contact us if you develop any of the above problems.

Figure 5:2 These signals are alerting you to a possible medical complication. Contact your clinician immediately if you notice any of these symptoms.

2. **YOU ARE IMPORTANT IN MAKING THE IUD SAFE AND EFFECTIVE** for you. Remember the danger signs, check your IUD strings, and do whatever you can do to reduce your own risks of infection or pregnancy. Read the section on *Tips For Success* for specific steps you can take.

COMMON CAUSES OF ACCIDENTAL PREGNANCY

1. **THE IUD HAS BEEN PARTIALLY OR COMPLETELY EXPELLED.** In some cases, cramping pain alerts the woman to this problem. But expulsion can be completely painless, and the woman may have no idea that the IUD has come out. Checking your IUD string is the only way to be sure.

2. **THE WOMAN HAS BECOME PREGNANT VERY SOON AFTER INSERTION** of her IUD. It is important to use condoms, foam, or another spermicide as a backup for your IUD during the first 3 months it is in place. Pregnancy is more likely to occur during this time than later on.

HAVING YOUR IUD INSERTED

Be sure you understand your clinician's ideas and feelings about when your IUD should be inserted. In some cases, an IUD can be inserted at your very first visit, although you will often need to plan a second visit for the insertion. Whenever possible, it is wise to have a culture for gonorrhea beforehand and to delay insertion for a few days until the culture results can be obtained.

Have someone come with you when you see our clinician for IUD insertion. If you have cramps or feel shaky or weak afterward, you will be glad to have company for your trip home. The insertion procedure does not take long, usually 5 or 10 minutes. Most women have cramps during insertion and for the first few hours afterward, but most say the pain is not severe. Some women have minimal or no discomfort during IUD insertion. You may want to take 2 or 3 aspirin tablets or 1 or 2 tablets of medication for menstrual cramps about one hour *before* your appointment.

Before the insertion, discuss with your clinician any questions you may have about the IUD, how it is inserted, and which IUD to use.

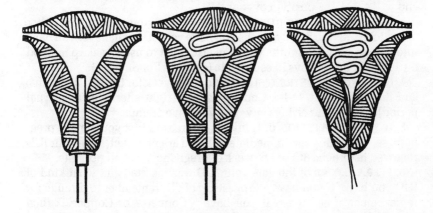

Figure 5:3 Insertion of an IUD into the uterus should be performed by an experienced clinician. You may have some cramps during and for a few hours after the insertion.

CHECKING FOR YOUR IUD STRING(S)

Use one or two fingers to locate your cervix. Your cervix feels like a firm round knob protruding from the roof of your vagina. Move your finger in a circular motion over the surface of your cervix. You will probably be able to feel the indentation in the center of your cervix where the cervical canal opens. Your IUD string (or strings) extends through the canal and about two inches into your vagina. An IUD string feels like fine nylon fishing line. When you check, be sure you *do not* feel firm plastic in the opening of the cervical canal.

If your string(s) feel longer, if you cannot find your string(s), or if you feel the firm plastic of your IUD itself, *see your clinician right away*. Be sure to use your backup method of birth control if you have intercourse.

INSTRUCTIONS FOR IUD USERS

1. IF YOU HAVE ANY OF THE IUD DANGER SIGNS, EVEN MILD ONES, SEE YOUR CLINICIAN RIGHT AWAY. Be especially alert for problems during the first few weeks you have your IUD.

2. RETURN TO YOUR CLINICIAN 2 to 6 weeks after your IUD is inserted for a checkup. Your clinician will be looking for any signs of early infection and will check the position of your IUD.

3. USE A BACKUP METHOD OF BIRTH CONTROL (condoms, foam, or another spermicide) for the first 3 months you have your IUD whenever you have intercourse. After 3 months you may also want to use a backup method during your fertile days in each cycle (see *Tips For Success*).

4. CHECK YOUR IUD STRING(S) at least once a week for the first 3 months, and then, after that, at least once a month (right after your menstrual period). Check your strings any time you have cramps.

5. IF YOU MISS A PERIOD, or think for any reason that you may be pregnant, see your clinician immediately. If you are pregnant, have your IUD removed before the 6th or 7th week of pregnancy, if at all possible.

6. KEEP A RECORD of the date your IUD was inserted and what kind of IUD you have. If you have a Progestasert IUD, remember to arrange for replacement after 1 year. If you have a Copper 7 or Copper T, then arrange for replacement after 3 years. Other IUD types remain effective as long as they are in place.

7. DO NOT TRY TO REMOVE YOUR IUD yourself. If you want to have it removed, see your clinician.

HAVING YOUR IUD REMOVED

Some clinicians feel it is easier to remove an IUD during the first 10 days or so of a menstrual cycle—during or soon after a normal period. It is possible, however, to remove an IUD at other times as well. If you are having infections or other problems, immediate removal may be important.

If your IUD is removed in the middle of the cycle, just before or after ovulation, then it may not provide birth control protection during that cycle. For this reason, it is important to avoid intercourse or to use your backup method of birth control for at least 7 days before IUD removal.

IUD removal can usually be done more quickly and less painfully than insertion.

PROBLEMS TO WATCH FOR

1. **HEAVY MENSTRUAL FLOW, PROLONGED FLOW, OR SPOTTING.** Although these problems are quite common and may not mean trouble, definitely discuss them with your clinician. Your clinician will need to be sure that you are not becoming anemic because of the increased bleeding caused by the IUD. Abnormal bleeding can be a sign of other serious problems including infection in the uterus and ectopic pregnancy (see below).

2. **CRAMPING AND PAIN.** Immediately after an IUD insertion, most women have some cramping which can last as long as 24 hours. Increased cramping during menstrual periods and at midcycle (during ovulation) are also common. If the cramping or pain is severe or prolonged (persisting continuously for more than 4 hours or so) then it is very important to see your clinician. Persistent pain can be a sign of uterine infection, and early medical treatment is important.

3. **INFECTION IN THE UTERUS.** Signs of infection may be persistent cramps or pain, abnormal bleeding or discharge, tenderness or pain during intercourse, fever, and feeling tired and run down. Often, when infection begins, the symptoms may be mild and only one or two symptoms may be present. Gonorrhea and other sexually transmitted bacteria are frequently the initial cause of infection. Infection can spread from your uterus up into your tubes or even into your abdominal cavity. *Do not wait. See your clinician right away.* Early treatment is the key to preventing very serious complications and permanent damage to your tubes. Damaged tubes can cause infertility. Infection may occur in 1 of every 300 to 1,000 users.

4. **PREGNANCY OR ECTOPIC (TUBAL) PREGNANCY.** See you clinician right away if you miss a menstrual period, if your period is late or unusually light, or if you have other signs of pregnancy such as breast tenderness, nausea, vomiting, and tiredness. If you are pregnant, you will want to have your IUD removed as soon as possible. At this time, your clinician will need to examine you carefully to be sure that you do not have an ectopic (tubal) pregnancy. Pregnancy with an IUD in place and ectopic pregnancy are serious problems: Miscarriage, severe infection, and internal hemorrhage bleeding are complications that can occur and can

lead to death if treatment is delayed. About 1 or 2 ectopic pregnancies occur in 1,000 IUD users each year.

5. **EXPULSION OF THE IUD.** Uterine contractions can partially expel an IUD into the cervix or completely out of the uterus and into the vagina. Often there are no symptoms which you would notice. Or, you may have some cramping, spotting or unusual discharge. If the IUD is not in proper position, it cannot protect against pregnancy. That is why it is important to check your strings regularly. Between 5 to 20% of users expel their IUD during the first year.

6. **LOST IUD STRING.** If your IUD strings are lost, you need to see your clinician. Most often the IUD string(s) has been drawn up into your cervix or uterus. Your clinician will first want to be sure you are not pregnant. If you are not, your clinician may be able to find the string in your cervix with little difficulty. Or, your clinician may simply remove the IUD and insert another one if you wish.

If your clinician is not able to find your string or your IUD easily, then you will need further evaluation to determine whether it has perforated (punctured) your uterus and entered your abdominal cavity (occurs in about 1 to 9 in 1,000 IUD users), or whether it is still in place in your uterus. Arrangements can then be made to remove your IUD.

7. **LONG IUD STRINGS.** If your IUD string(s) seems significantly longer (extends more than 2 inches or so from your cervix), see your clinician right away and use a backup method of birth control in the meantime. It may be that the IUD has been partially expelled downward into your cervix. If you have a Copper 7 IUD, long strings may just mean that the extra loop of string that this particular device uses has moved from the uterus down through the cervix. In any case, your clinician needs to check your IUD.

8. **VAGINAL DISCHARGE OR ODOR.** Excessive vaginal discharge or odor can be caused by an IUD. Be sure to see your clinician because these symptoms can mean serious uterine infection. If there is no evidence of uterine infection then antibiotic treatment is often successful in treating the odor/discharge problem.

9. **PARTNER DISCOMFORT.** Irritation of your partner's penis during or after intercourse can be a problem if your IUD string is too long, too short, or knotted. Your clinician may be able to help by trimming the string.

TIPS FOR SUCCESS

1. **MEMORIZE THE IUD DANGER SIGNS.** See you clinician immediately even if your symptoms are not severe.

2. **DO WHATEVER YOU CAN TO AVOID GONORRHEA** and other sexually transmitted infections. Change your mind about "intercourse tonight," or have your partner use condoms, if you have the least doubt. If your partner has a penile discharge or sores you can see, you again ought to change your mind about intercourse tonight. Any time you have more than one partner, or for the first few months with a new partner, you may want to rely on condoms. With more than one partner, your chances of being exposed to gonorrhea are higher.

3. **CHOOSE A CLINICIAN WHO IS EXPERIENCED WITH THE IUD.** If you move, find a new clinician right away. You can call Planned Parenthood or your local health department for a referral.

4. **HAVE A BACKUP METHOD ON HAND.** If you use a backup method for the first 3 months you have your IUD and then during your fertile days each cycle, you will have a method with 99% effectiveness. And you will greatly reduce the risks of serious complications. Condoms, spermicides, or a diaphragm used with spermicides reduce your risk of infections as well as your risk of pregnancy.

GO BACK TO YOUR CLINICIAN

1. **IF YOU HAVE ANY OF THE DANGER SIGNS:**
   - Cramps, pelvic pain, or painful intercourse
   - Unusual bleeding or discharge
   - Missed period or other signs of pregnancy
   - Fever or chills
   - Missing string(s).

2. **IF YOU THINK YOU MAY HAVE BEEN EXPOSED TO GONORRHEA** or another sexually transmitted infection.

3. **IF YOUR STRING IS LONGER, OR IF YOU FEEL FIRM PLASTIC** in your cervical canal.

4. **WHEN YOU NEED TO HAVE YOUR IUD REPLACED:** Progestasert users, after 1 year; Copper 7 and Copper T users, after 3 years.

5. **FOR ROUTINE EXAMS** every 6 to 12 months to confirm that your IUD is in proper position and that you have no signs of infection.

CHAPTER 6: DIAPHRAGM

The diaphragm is a very safe and effective method provided you use it correctly. This chapter describes how to use the diaphragm so that it will give you the best protection possible. To learn more about the diaphragm and to see how it compares with other birth control methods, read Chapter 1.

BEFORE YOU BEGIN using the diaphragm, think about the following questions. If you have any YES answers, be sure to discuss them with your clinician.

YES/NO   Am I allergic or sensitive to rubber (latex) or spermicide?

YES/NO   Do I have any doubts about my ability to insert the diaphragm or check for proper placement?

YES/NO   Do I have problems with repeated bladder (urine) infections?

IMPORTANT THINGS TO REMEMBER

1. BE SURE YOUR DIAPHRAGM IS IN PLACE (WITH SPERMICIDE) EVERY TIME you have intercourse.

2. IF YOU HAVE TROUBLE, GO BACK TO YOUR CLINICIAN. Many times problems can be resolved by a change in the diaphragm or rim type (of the diaphragm), or a change in spermicide. Or, you may decide to use another method.

COMMON CAUSES OF ACCIDENTAL PREGNANCY

1. TRYING TO GUESS ABOUT SAFE DAYS. If you want to combine the fertility awareness method and the diaphragm method, then you will need to be careful and consistent about your calendar records and calculations. Otherwise, use your diaphragm all the time, including during your menstrual period.

2. FORGETTING TO TAKE THE DIAPHRAGM ON YOUR VACATION. Double check to be sure you have your diaphragm and spermicide with you before you leave for a vacation or weekend away from home.

LEARNING TO INSERT AND REMOVE YOUR DIAPHRAGM

Be sure you practice inserting your diaphragm when you have your exam and diaphragm fitting. After you have inserted your diaphragm, your clinician can check to see that it is in the correct position.

For insertion you can stand with one foot propped up (on the edge of a bathtub or toilet), squat, or lie on your back.

TO INSERT YOUR DIAPHRAGM, hold it with the dome down and press the opposite sides of the rim together so that it folds. Use your other hand to spread apart the lips of your vagina and guide the diaphragm. Push the diaphragm downward and back along the back wall of your vagina as far as it will go. Then tuck the front rim upward behind your pubic bone.

When it is in the correct position, your diaphragm should be comfortable. If you can feel it, or if you have discomfort, then it is probably *not in the correct position.* Try taking it out and reinserting it.

Next, **CHECK THE PLACEMENT** of your diaphragm. When correctly placed, the back rim of the diaphragm is below and behind the cervix,

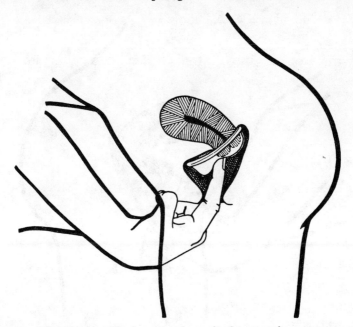

Figure 6:1   When checking the placement of your diaphragm, make sure your cervix is covered and the diaphragm is securely in place. You should not be able to feel your diaphragm if it is in the correct position.

and the front rim is tucked up behind the pubic bone. Use your index finger to locate your cervix. Your cervix should be *covered* by the soft rubber dome of the diaphragm. Then check to be sure the front rim is snugly in place behind your pubic bone. Often it is not possible to feel the back rim of the diaphragm.

If you have trouble finding your cervix, first try to locate it without your diaphragm in place. Use one or two fingers to locate the roof of your vagina, then follow the roof back until you reach a round, firm donut-shaped protrusion.

TO REMOVE YOUR DIAPHRAGM, use one finger to hook the front rim of the diaphragm, or slip one finger behind the front rim (between the diaphragm rim and the pubic bone), then pull the rim downward and out. If you find it hard to remove your diaphragm, try squatting and pushing downward with your abdominal muscles. In other words, bear down as though you were having a bowel movement.

When you actually use your diaphragm for contraception, you will put spermicidal jelly or cream inside the dome of the diaphragm before you insert it. (Read Chapter 8 on spermicides.)

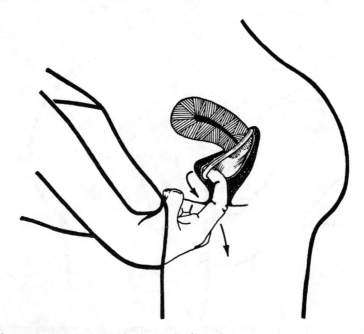

Figure 6:2   To remove your diaphragm, hook one finger underneath the front rim and pull downward.

TO APPLY SPERMICIDE, hold the diaphragm with the dome down (like a cup). Squeeze about one tablespoon of jelly or cream from the tube into the dome. Spread a little bit of the jelly or cream around the rim of the diaphragm with your finger. Next, press the opposite sides of the rim together so that the diaphragm folds with the spermicide on the inside of the dome. Now it is ready for insertion. When you insert the diaphragm, the spermicidal cream or jelly inside the dome should be facing your cervix. The side of the dome without spermicide should be facing the opening of your vagina.

A plastic inserter is available for use with the *coil spring diaphragm.* (This type of diaphragm is also easy to insert by hand.) If you are using an inserter, first apply spermicidal cream or jelly on your diaphragm, just as you would if you were inserting it by hand. Then fold the diaphragm and hook the front and back rims on the inserter. The spermicide should be on the side facing up and away from the inserter. Use the inserter to guide the diaphragm into the opening of your vagina, then downward and back along the back wall of your vagina. When your diaphragm is entirely inside and the inserter has reached the deepest part of the vagina, twist the inserter to release the diaphragm, and remove the inserter. Finally, use your finger to check the placement of your diaphragm.

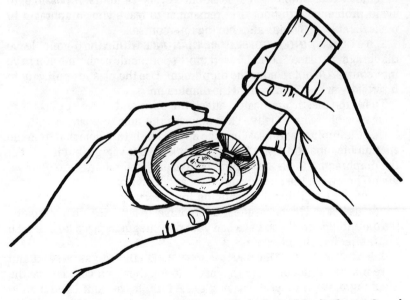

Figure 6:3 Sperm-killing cream or jelly goes inside the dome of the diaphragm. Spread the spermicide over the entire surface of the dome, including the rim.

USING YOUR DIAPHRAGM

1. **BE SURE YOUR DIAPHRAGM WITH SPERMICIDAL CREAM OR JELLY IS IN PLACE EACH TIME YOU HAVE INTERCOURSE.** You can insert your diaphragm just before intercourse, or ahead of time. So far, there are no conclusive studies to show just how long spermicide retains full activity, how long the diaphragm must be left in place after intercourse, or whether use of extra spermicide is necessary for repeated intercourse. One of the most comprehensive studies or diaphragm users showed very excellent effectiveness when users inserted the diaphragm any time up to 6 hours before intercourse. It may be that an even longer interval would also be fine.

The following rules use traditional time limits. But, remember that the most important thing is having your diaphragm in place, covering your cervix—not in your drawer. So, if you need to bend the time limits, do that rather than "take a chance" just once.

2. **AFTER INTERCOURSE, LEAVE YOUR DIAPHRAGM IN PLACE FOR AT LEAST 6 TO 8 HOURS.** Do not douche during that time. Then remove the diaphragm when it is convenient. If you are going to have intercourse again, wash the diaphragm, apply new spermicidal jelly or cream, and reinsert it. Try to remove your diaphragm at least once every 24 hours, if possible, to avoid problems with odor. But remember to leave your diaphragm in place for at least 6 hours after having intercourse.

3. **IF YOU HAVE INTERCOURSE MORE THAN ONCE** within the 6-hour "leave diaphragm in place" period, insert more spermicide each time you have intercourse. *Do not remove the diaphragm.* Use the plastic applicator to insert jelly or cream in front of the diaphragm.

To fill the plastic applicator, attach the open end of the applicator to your tube of cream or jelly. Then squeeze the tube to push spermicide inside the applicator tube. When the applicator is full, detach it from the spermicide tube and insert it into the back of your vagina (but in front of the diaphragm). Push in the plunger to squirt spermicide into your vagina. Then wash the plastic applicator and let it dry.

If you find additional spermicide too messy, you may want to use condoms instead for subsequent intercourse. In any case, *do not remove the diaphragm* until you have had your diaphragm in place for at least 6 hours after having intercourse.

4. **IF YOU HAVE HAD YOUR DIAPHRAGM IN PLACE FOR 6 HOURS OR MORE** and have not had intercourse in the last 6 hours, then you can remove the diaphragm, wash it, let it dry, and place it in its case until you plan to have intercourse again.

TAKING CARE OF YOUR DIAPHRAGM

1. BE SURE YOU HAVE THE SUPPLIES YOU WILL NEED at home—or with you when you are traveling:
- a diaphragm in a plastic case
- 1 or 2 tubes of spermicidal jelly or cream
- a plastic applicator for inserting extra spermicide

Brands of spermicidal cream and jelly differ in chemical composition, perfume, and price. They are all similar in effectiveness. You may prefer the more lubricating effect of jelly or the somewhat more pleasant smell of cream. You do not need a prescription to buy spermicidal jelly or cream.

2. USE PLAIN, MILD SOAP AND WATER TO WASH YOUR DIAPHRAGM, then dry it with a towel and put it in its case. You can use cornstarch to dust your diaphragm if you wish, but do not use talcum powder or perfumed powder. Store your case away from heat (not near a radiator or heater).

3. CHECK YOUR DIAPHRAGM FOR TEARS OR HOLES each time you use it. Hold it up to the light and stretch the dome slightly to see any defects.

4. YOUR DIAPHRAGM SHOULD NOT INTERFERE WITH NORMAL ACTIVITIES. Urination or a bowel movement should not affect the diaphragm's position, but you can check its placement afterward if you wish. It is fine to shower or bathe with the diaphragm in place

5. KEEP YOUR DIAPHRAGM AWAY FROM PETROLEUM PRODUCTS. Vaseline or some vaginal medications contain petroleum, which can damage the latex of the diaphragm. If you want to use a lubricant, choose one of the water soluble lubricants, such as KY Jelly, Personal Lubricant, H-R Lubricating Jelly or Surgilube. The following medications do not contain petroleum: Candeption ointment, Candeption capsules, Vanobid ointment, AVC Cream, Aci Jel, Monistat Cream, Koro-Sulf Cream, Myocostatin Tablets, Nilstat Tablets, Korostatin Tablets, Premarin Cream, Sultrin Cream, and Vanobid Tablets. Ask you clinician whether using your diaphragm or having intercourse will be a problem whenever you are treated for vaginal problems.

PROBLEMS TO WATCH FOR

1. PELVIC DISCOMFORT, CRAMPS, OR PRESSURE ON THE BLADDER OR RECTUM. If your diaphragm is not comfortable, or if you have pain or cramps during or after intercourse, it may mean that your diaphragm fits too snugly. Often these problems can be eliminated by switching to a

smaller diaphragm size or to a different type of diaphragm rim. Be sure to see your clinician. Similar symptoms can also mean a serious medical problem, such as pelvic infection.

2. IRRITATION OR BURNING FROM SPERMICIDE. Brands of jelly or cream differ in chemical composition. It is often possible to find a brand that is not irritating. If you have difficulty, see your clinician for suggestions about alternative brands and to be sure that your irritation is not caused by a vaginal infection.

3. BLADDER INFECTION OR KIDNEY INFECTION. Bladder infections are common and can occur whether or not you are using the diaphragm. In a small number of diaphragm users, however, excessive pressure from the diaphragm against the urethra (the tube that empties urine from the bladder) can lead to repeated episodes of bladder infection or kidney infection. Again, a change in diaphragm size or rim type (of the diaphragm) may correct the problem. Sometimes, however, a change to another method of birth control is needed.

TIPS FOR SUCCESS

1. WHEN YOU FIRST GET YOUR DIAPHRAGM, practice inserting it and removing it several times each day for the first few days. Then you will be confident that you can do it easily and correctly.

2. TRY TO FIND YOUR OWN STYLE for using the diaphragm. For example, some women find it easiest to make diaphragm insertion a routine— inserting it every night after work or every night at bedtime. Some couples share responsibility for keeping supplies on hand and being sure the diaphragm is in place. Sometimes the man puts the diaphragm in for his wife or partner.

3. IF YOU TRAVEL OFTEN, or if you use your diaphragm frequently, you may want to have 2 diaphragms. Also be sure to have on hand an extra tube of jelly or cream.

4. TO BE AN EXTRA-EFFECTIVE USER PAY ATTENTION TO THE POSITION OF YOUR DIAPHRAGM during intercourse and afterward. If your partner's penis dislodges the diaphragm or slips between the front rim of the diaphragm and your pubic bone, the effectiveness of your method is reduced. This is not at all likely, but it can happen especially if your lovemaking involves multiple, rapid penetrations and withdrawals or the female superior position. You can use your fingers to guide your partner's penis toward the back wall of your vagina. After intercourse, check the placement of your diaphragm. If it is not in correct position

then immediately insert an extra application of spermicidal jelly. Discuss this problem with your clinician. You may want to consider morning-after treatment. Your clinician will want to check your diaphragm size to be sure you have the snuggist fit possible and that your insertion technique is correct.

GO BACK TO YOUR CLINICIAN

1. If you have any doubt about your ability to insert your diaphragm correctly, or about its fit.

2. If you have an irritation, discomfort, or cramps during or after diaphragm use, or at other times.

3. If you have bladder infection symptoms such as frequent urination, pain or bleeding with urination, an urgent need to urinate, or if you have kidney infection symptoms such as back pain, fever, chills, or cloudy or bloody urine.

4. If you menstrual period is late or you suspect for any reason that you may be pregnant.

5. If you are considering morning-after treatment because you have had intercourse without your diaphragm.

6. If you need to have your diaphragm size checked: after pregnancy, or after surgery involving the vagina.

7. If your diaphragm is not in correct position after intercourse, or if you think it may have been dislodged during intercourse, you might want to consider morning-after treatment. Also, your clinician can check the size of your diaphragm to be sure it fits properly.

CHAPTER 7: CONDOMS (RUBBERS)

There are really no key questions you need to ask yourself before using a condom for the first time because there are no serious medical complications caused by condoms. Some men and women are sensitive or allergic to latex and develop irritations or a rash if they continue to use latex condoms. This is quite rare, however, and a change to natural skin condoms may solve the problem.

IMPORTANT THINGS TO REMEMBER

1. USE YOUR CONDOMS EVERY TIME you have intercourse.
2. BE SURE THE CONDOM IS PUT ON BEFORE the penis is put in or near the vagina.

CAUSES OF ACCIDENTAL PREGNANCY

1. TRYING TO GUESS ABOUT SAFE DAYS. If you want to combine the fertility awareness method with the condom method, then you will need to be careful and consistent about your calendar records and calculations as to when ovulation occurs. Otherwise, use condoms all the time, including during menstrual periods.

2. FORGETTING TO HAVE CONDOMS HANDY. Be sure you have a supply of condoms handy—or take time to stop at the drugstore. Double check that you have remembered condoms before you leave for a vacation or weekend away from home. Don't let yourself say, "just this once."

3. THE CONDOM SLIPPED OFF AND SPILLED in or near the vagina after ejaculation. The penis returns to its normal size soon after intercourse, and the condom can slip off. This is why it is important for the man to hold the top of the condom and withdraw carefully soon after ejaculation.

4. THE CONDOM BROKE OR TORE. Actually, this is not a common problem unless you are using very old, britle condoms. Having on hand a backup spermicide (such as foam, jelly, or cream) can be a lifesaver in this

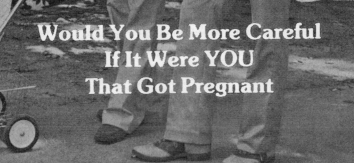

Would You Be More Careful If It Were YOU That Got Pregnant

(To obtain copies of this poster contact the Family Planning Program, Grady Memorial Hospital, 80 Butler St., SE, Atlanta, GA 30335)

situation. Insert an applicator full of spermicide into the vagina as soon as possible. Otherwise, try a plain, warm water douche right away; it probably will help to provide some protection. You may want to get in touch with your clinician within 24 hours or so to discuss morning-after emergency birth control measures.

HOW TO GET CONDOMS

Your local health department, family planning clinic, Planned Parenthood clinic, or venereal disease clinic is likely to have condoms available free or at a low cost.

Condoms are sold (no prescription is needed) at most drugstores, many grocery and discount stores, in vending machines, and by mail order in national magazines.

DO MALES PRACTICE BIRTH CONTROL? YES!

In a recent issue of *Worldwatch* on "Men and Family Planning," Bruce Stokes observed that, worldwide, one in three people using birth control rely on a male method. About 37 million men use condoms, 35 million have had vasectomies, and millions more rely on withdrawal. "One out of five Americans, one out of two Italians, and four out of five Japanese use a male method of birth control regularly," Stokes says.

Each of the major female methods of birth control has 50 to 65 million users worldwide.

Despite the fact that less than one percent of the people who visit birth control clinics in the United States are men, Stokes claims that many more American males **ARE** interested in and **DO** take responsibility for birth control.

COUPLES' PRACTICE OF MALE CONTRACEPTION:

	Withdrawal	Condom	Vasectomy	Total
France	17.6	5.0	0.1	22.7
Great Britain	6.0	16.0	6.0	
Italy	29.0	16.0		45.0
Japan	5.1	78.9	1.3	85.3
Poland	30.0	10.0		40.0
United States				
ALL	2.0	7.2	10.5	19.7
TEENS (15-19)	18.8	23.2		42.2

Stokes, Bruce, "Men and Family Planning," *WORLDWATCH PAPER 41*, Dec. 1980, p. 12.

There are several different types of condoms and many brands. Latex condoms are available plain or lubricated, and must meet federal standards for strength and thickness. Natural skin condoms are regulated in exactly the same manner; some men feel they offer better sensitivity. Condoms are usually packaged 3 to a box.

USING CONDOMS EFFECIVELY

1. **USE A CONDOM EVERY TIME** you have intercourse and be sure it is in place before the penis is put in or near the vagina.

2. **LEAVE ROOM AT THE TIP** of the condom for semen. Some condoms have a reservoir at the tip. If the condom you are using does not have a reservoir tip, pinch the end with your fingers as you roll the condom onto the penis.

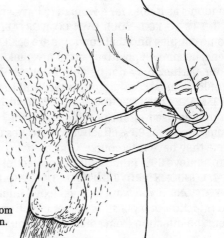

Figure 7:1 When putting on a condom leave a little space at the tip for semen.

3. **HAVE ON HAND BACKUP SPERMICIDE (FOAM, CREAM, OR JELLY)** for emergencies. If a condom slips off, spills, or breaks inside the vagina, or you see a leak after intercourse, insert an applicator-full of foam, jelly, or cream into the vagina **IMMEDIATELY.** (Read Chapter 8 on spermicides.)

4. **DON'T LET THE CONDOM SLIP OFF** the penis after intercourse. As the penis returns to normal size, the condom will be looser. Hold onto the condom rim during withdrawal, and be sure withdrawal occurs before erection subsides completely.

5. **AFTER INTERCOURSE, CHECK THE CONDOM FOR LEAKS** or tears before your throw it away.

6. AVOID PETROLEUM jellies such as Vaseline if you are using condoms. Petroleum may deteriorate latex. You CAN USE water-soluble lubricants such as KY jelly, H-R Lubricating Jelly, Surgilube, or Personal lubricant, or a spermicidal jelly if you want extra lubrication.

7. STORE CONDOMS IN A COOL PLACE. If you keep them in their original packages at room temperature, away from heat sources, vents, or radiators, condoms should last about 5 years.

TIPS FOR SUCCESS

1. USING CONDOMS THE FIRST TIME, or in a new relationship, is often the hardest step. Maybe you can think of something lighthearted but loving to say as you reach for a condom. "I know this is your favorite color.... " It certainly makes as much sense for a woman or man to be prepared with condoms as it does for a woman to have an IUD or to be taking Pills.

2. TRY TO FIND YOUR OWN COMFORTABLE STYLE for using condoms. Some couples find that condoms are easier to use if putting them on the penis becomes a positive part of lovemaking. Try to talk to your partner. Your partner may not be able to guess what you are feeling, or what would be most comfortable or pleasant to you.

3. MANY COUPLES CHOOSE TO USE CONDOMS ALONG WITH A SPERMICIDE. Condoms used alone provide excellent birth control protection: Condoms are about 98% effective for couples using condoms correctly each time they have intercourse. Couples who use foam along with condoms can achieve 99% (almost 100%) protection.

4. CONDOMS PROVIDE PROTECTION AGAINST SEXUALLY TRANSMISSIBLE INFECTIONS. If you want to have sexual intercourse with a person who has an infection or a possible risk of infection, use condoms. They can prevent the infection from spreading to you.

GO BACK TO YOUR CLINICIAN

1. IF YOU HAVE AN IRRITATION or an allergic reaction, or find for any reason you are not able to use condoms as you had planned. You need to think about an alternative birth control method.

2. IF YOU FIND YOU ARE TAKING CHANCES—"just this once." Another birth control option may better meet your needs.

3. IF YOU SUSPECT PREGNANCY because of a late menstrual period, tiredness, breast tenderness, nausea, or another sign of pregnancy.

CHAPTER 8: VAGINAL SPERMICIDES: FOAM, SUPPOSITORIES, TABLETS, CREAM AND JELLY

There are really no key questions you need to ask yourself before using foam, spermicidal suppositories, foaming tablets, or contraceptive cream or jelly. There are presently no known serious medical complications caused by these products. Some men and women are sensitive or allergic to spermicidal agents or other chemicals in certain products and develop an irritation or a rash if they use them. This is quite rare, however, and changing to another brand may solve the problem.

IMPORTANT THINGS TO REMEMBER

1. USE YOUR SPERMICIDE EVERY TIME you have intercourse.

2. BE SURE THE SPERMICIDE IS IN PLACE IN YOUR VAGINA BEFORE the penis is put in or near the vagina.

COMMON CAUSES OF ACCIDENTAL PREGNANCY

1. TRYING TO GUESS ABOUT SAFE DAYS. If you want to combine the fertility awareness method with a spermicide method then you will need to be careful and consistent about your calendar records and calculations as to when ovulation occurs. Otherwise, use spermicide all the time, including during menstrual periods.

2. FORGETTING TO HAVE SPERMICIDE ON HAND. Be sure you have on hand a supply of spermicide—take time to stop at the drugstore. Double check that you have remembered to bring your spermicide before you leave for a vacation or weekend away from home. Don't let yourself say "just this once."

3. **NOT QUITE FOLLOWING DIRECTIONS FOR THE PRODUCT.** It is essential to allow time for a foaming tablet to foam or a suppository to melt, and to realize that protection from 1 application of foam lasts for only 30 minutes or 1 act of intercourse. These products provide greatest effectiveness only when you read and follow the directions carefully.

CHOOSING A SPERMICIDE PRODUCT

The various types of spermicide products available differ in chemical composition, effectiveness, and instructions for use. *Foam, cream, and jelly* all must be inserted into the vagina with a plastic applicator prior to intercourse. Of these three, *foam is probably the most effective,* with cream alone second and jelly alone third. Since these methods are otherwise similar it makes sense to choose foam, unless you are using spermicide with a diaphragm.

Contraceptive suppositories and foaming tablets are newer products, and comparative effectiveness rates are not definite. Most clinicians feel that their effectiveness is similar to foam, or perhaps just a little lower. However, you may find them more convenient to use, since they are small, lightweight, and a plastic applicator is not necessary. (They do seem ideal for backpacking or weekend travel.)

HOW TO GET VAGINAL SPERMICIDES

Your local health department, family planning clinics, Planned Parenthood clinic, or venereal disease clinic is likely to have foam, and possibly other spermicidal products, available free or at low cost.

Spermicides are sold (no prescription is needed) at most drugstores, many grocery and discount stores, and by mail order in national magazines.

USING FOAM EFFECTIVELY

1. **USE FOAM EVERY TIME** you have intercourse. Be sure it is in place before the penis is put in or near the vagina.

2. **TO INSERT FOAM,** first shake the can vigorously 20 or 30 times. Next, fill the plastic applicator and insert it deep into your vagina. Push the plunger to expel the foam. Use 1 or 2 full applicators, according to directions on the foam can.

Figure 8:1 Correct placement of spermicide. Insert foam deep into the vagina so that it covers your cervix.

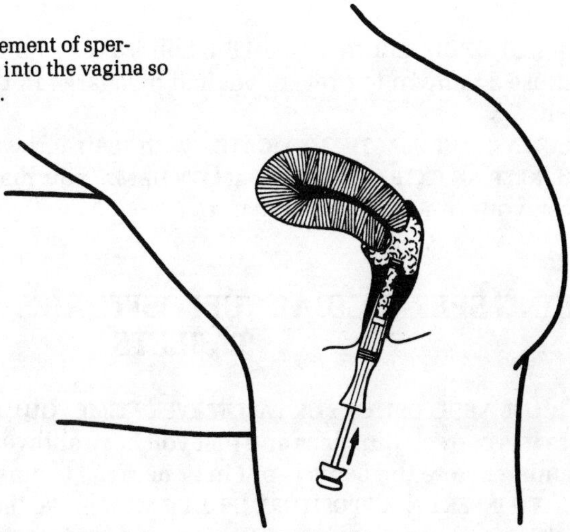

Figure 8:2 Incorrect placement of spermicide. This foam is not covering the cervix and will not provide maximal protection against pregnancy.

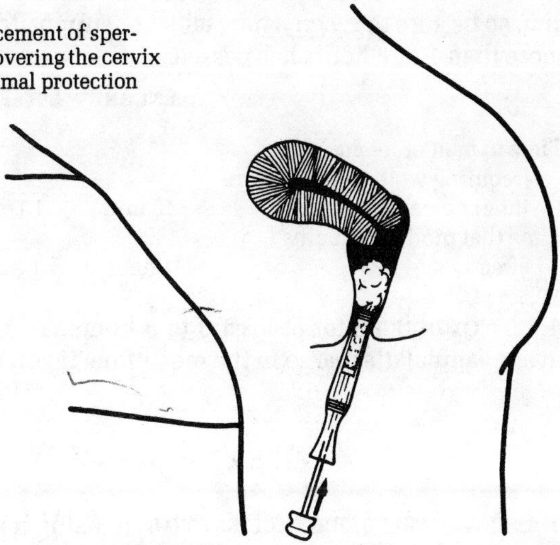

3. **INSERT A NEW DOSE OF FOAM** (1 or 2 full applicators) **EACH TIME YOU HAVE INTERCOURSE**. Foam protection last 30 minutes, so be sure you have inserted foam *no more than 30 minutes beforehand*. Use a new dose just before a repeated act of intercourse or if more than 30 minutes has passed.

71

4. **DO NOT DOUCHE** for at least 6-8 hours after your last intercourse. You can use a tampon to prevent vaginal discharge in the meantime, if you wish.

5. **WASH THE PLASTIC APPLICATOR** with soap and water after you use it.

6. **KEEP AN EXTRA CAN OF FOAM ON HAND.** You may not be able to tell when your can is about to run out.

USING SPERMICIDAL SUPPOSITORIES AND FOAMING TABLETS

1. **USE A SUPPOSITORY OR TABLET EVERY TIME YOU HAVE INTERCOURSE.** Be sure it is correctly in place and that you have allowed time for melting or foaming before the penis is put in or near the vagina.

2. **TO INSERT A SUPPOSITORY OR TABLET,** remove it completely from the package and use your fingers to guide it deep into your vagina. It should rest against or near your cervix.

3. **INSERT A NEW TABLET OR SUPPOSITORY EACH TIME YOU HAVE INTER-COURSE.** Protection lasts 1 or 2 hours depending on the brand you are using, so be sure to insert a new tablet or suppository before intercourse if more than 1 or 2 hours has passed.

	ENCARE	INTERCEPT	SEMICIDE
Time to melt or foam: (required waiting time before intercourse)	10 min	10 min	15 min
Time that product remains effective:	1 hour	1 hour	1 hour

4. **DO NOT DOUCHE** for at least 6 to 8 hours. You can use a tampon to prevent vaginal discharge in the meantime, if you wish.

TIPS FOR SUCCESS

1. **USING A SPERMICIDE THE FIRST TIME,** or using it in a new relationship, is often the hardest step. To lessen any awkwardness maybe you can think of something lighthearted but loving to say as you reach for the foam can. "I know this is your favorite color.... " Using a spermicide certainly makes as much sense as having an IUD or taking Pills.

2. **TRY TO FIND YOUR OWN COMFORTABLE STYLE** for using spermicide. Some couples find spermicide is easier to use when it becomes a positive

part of lovemaking. If the taste of spermicide is bothersome, wait until after oral sex to insert it. Try to talk to your partner. Your partner may not be able to guess what you are feeling or what would be most comfortable or pleasant to you.

3. **MANY COUPLES CHOOSE TO USE SPERMICIDE ALONG WITH CONDOMS.** Spermicide used alone can provide excellent birth control protection: About 98% effectiveness for couples using spermicide correctly each time they have intercourse. Couples who use condoms along with spermicide can achieve 99% (almost 100%) protection. Just as effective as birth control Pills.

"FOAMANDCONDOMS"

"Foamandcondoms" is not one word.

Occasionally, women have walked into doctors' offices asking for the method "foamandcondoms," unaware that it is two methods, not just one. Many providers and users of foam and of condoms link these two contraceptives together and think that either alone is ineffective. And for some couples, these two methods *are* ineffective when used alone.

However, many individuals have found out that foam alone *can* be effective as a contraceptive if it is used consistently and correctly. The same is true of condoms. The problem really is people. They tend to be careless in using foam, condoms, and other intercourse related methods.

Although these methods are effective when used alone, **remember,** using birth control methods in combination will provide extra protection against pregnancy.

GO BACK TO YOUR CLINICIAN

1. **IF YOU HAVE AN IRRITATION OR AN ALLERGIC REACTION,** or if you find, for any reason, that you are not able to use spermicide as you had planned. You need to think about an alternative birth control method.

2. **IF YOU FIND YOU ARE TAKING CHANCES** "just this once." Another birth control method may better meet your needs.

3. **IF YOU SUSPECT PREGNANCY** because of a late menstrual period, tiredness, breast tenderness, nausea.

CHAPTER 9: FERTILITY AWARENESS METHODS

As with any birth control method, fertility awareness methods have both advantages and disadvantages. The most serious disadvantage is the potential for an unplanned pregnancy to occur. Read Chapter 1 to learn more about the advantages of fertility awareness methods and to see how they compare with other methods of birth control.

BEFORE YOU BEGIN USING fertility awareness methods, think about the following questions. If you have any YES answers, be sure to discuss them with your clinician.

YES/NO   Does the length of my menstrual cycles vary by more than a few days from month to month?

YES/NO   Am I willing to abstain from sexual intercourse or find alternatives or sexual gratification?

YES/NO   Do I have trouble keeping track of or charting my menstrual cycles?

YES/NO   Is sexual spontaneity an important part of my sexual style?

YES/NO   Do I have a history of not ovulating?

IMPORTANT THINGS TO REMEMBER

1. CONSISTENT RECORDS AND CAREFUL CALCULATIONS ARE ESSENTIAL. Learning to interpret your charts may not be easy. Try to find a good class on fertility awareness or, while you are learning, work with a clinician experienced in this area.

2. IF IN DOUBT, ABSTAIN OR USE YOUR BACKUP METHOD. Whenever you are not absolutely sure about your cycle, or your signs don't quite make sense or fit, assume you are fertile.

3. ANY BIRTH CONTROL METHODS USED TOGETHER WILL GIVE YOU MORE PROTECTION against pregnancy. This is particularly true for fertility awareness methods.

4. DON'T RELY ON FERTILITY AWARENESS METHODS FOR BIRTH CONTROL UNTIL you have completed several cycles of careful record-keeping. Ideally, your clinician or instructor can help you review your records to be sure you are interpreting them accurately.

COMMON CAUSES OF ACCIDENTAL PREGNANCY

1. **HAVING INTERCOURSE JUST BEFORE SIGNS OF OVULATION BEGIN.** By far the most common cause of accidental pregnancy for couples using fertility awareness methods is having intercourse during or just after a menstrual period (during the supposed "early safe days"). Basal body temperature and mucus signs often do not give enough advance warning. Intercourse on Monday means sperm may still be present on Wednesday or even later, so mucus changes on Tuesday are too late to be meaningful. If you have some short cycles (less than 28 days), then you may have no "early safe days" at all! Couples who abstain from intercourse until after ovulation in each cycle have the highest effectiveness rates with fertility awareness methods.

2. **HAVING SEXUAL INTERCOURSE DURING YOUR FERTILE DAYS.** Many couples find it extremely difficult to determine the woman's fertile days. Others realize that she is fertile yet fail to abstain. Having intercourse during mid-cycle, when you are ovulating and when you are fertile, will **OFTEN** lead to pregnancy.

3. **FAILING TO CHART YOUR CYCLES PROPERLY.** Losing track of your menstrual cycle or failing to record information correctly can cause you to miscalculate your fertile period. Be sure to write down all the signals your body sends. Eliminating information or skipping a few days between charting may confuse you, and lead to miscalculation.

USING FERTILITY AWARENESS METHODS

During your fertile days you can choose to avoid all sexual activity, avoid only intercourse and enjoy other sexual activity, or continue to have intercourse while you use a backup method of birth control such as foam, condoms, or a diaphragm. Do whichever you and your partner choose.

Always use **YOUR MOST RECENT 8** cycles to make your calculations.

If your cycles begin to vary widely in length and you have many more fertile days than safe days, call your clinic or fertility awareness counselor. You may need to consider another method of birth control. Always bring your menstrual calendar and other cycle records with you when you visit your clinician or fertility awareness counselor

HOW TO USE THE CALENDAR METHOD

1. On the day your menstrual period starts, check your 8 most recent cycles as marked on your calendar. (A *cycle* begins on Day 1 of your

menstrual period and ends on the day before your next period starts.)
Find the longest and shortest of your 8 cycles.

2. Look at the fertile days chart below. Use your shortest cycle to find
your first fertile day. Use your longest cycle to find your last fertile day.
(For example, if your shortest cycle has been 22 days, your first fertile
day will be Day 4. If your longest cycle has been 28 days, your last fertile
day will be Day 17.)

3. Next, find out the dates for your fertile days for this coming cycle.
Start counting forward from the first day of your current menstrual
period. (For example, if your period starts September 6 and the chart
says your first fertile day will be Day 4, that means your first fertile day
will be September 9. If your last fertile day will be Day 17, that means
your last fertile day this month will be September 22. In this example,
your fertile days are September 9 through September 22.)

If your shortest cycle has been:	Your first fertile day is:	If your longest cycle has been:	Your last fertile day is:
21	3rd Day	21	10th Day
22	4th	22	11th
23	5th	23	12th
24	6th	24	13th
25	7th	25	14th
26	8th	26	15th
27	9th	27	16th
28	10th	28	17th
29	11th	29	18th
30	12th	30	19th
31	13th	31	20th
32	14th	32	21st
33	15th	33	22nd
34	16th	34	23rd
35	17th	35	24th

Day 1 = First day of menstrual bleeding

Figure 9:1 How to calculate your fertile period.
(Reprinted from *My Body, My Health*, John Wiley & Sons, Inc.)

HOW TO USE THE BASAL BODY TEMPERATURE METHOD

The basal body temperature (BBT) is by definition the lowest temperature reached by the body of a healthy person during waking hours. A fertile woman's resting or basal body temperature (BBT) normally *rises right after she ovulates.* Her temperature remains higher until her next menstrual period begins. Most women find that if they check and record their temperature every day, they can observe the temperature change that means ovulation has occurred.

1. If possible, use a special basal body temperature thermometer (BBT), rather than a fever thermometer. Thermometers and blank charts are sold in drugstores and are usually available at family planning clinics.

2. Take your temperature *each and every morning before* you get out of bed, and *before* you smoke a cigarette or begin any kind of activity. Take a reading after 5 full minutes. You can use the BBT thermometer orally or rectally, whichever you choose, but you must pick one site and take your temperature consistently every day.

3. Record your temperature every day on a special BBT chart. Connect the dots for each day so you can see a line going from Day 1 to Day 2 to Day 3, etc. (see Figure 9.2)

4. Your BBT will probably rise about 0.4–0.8 degrees as soon as you have ovulated. From then on, until your next period begins, it should stay elevated above your pre-ovulation temperatures.

5. Many women notice that their BBT drops about 24 hours before it begins to rise after ovulation. Other women have no drop in temperature at all. A drop in BBT probably means ovulation will occur within the next 24 hours.

6. Your BBT rises only AFTER ovulation, so if you had intercourse just before or during ovulation you wouldn't know it in time. Therefore, the safest way to use the BBT method is to avoid intercourse or use a backup method of brith control all through the first part of your cycle. You can assume your fertile days are over *only when your BBT has risen and has remained elevated for 3 full days.* For your BBT pattern to be clear-cut, all 3 days should have higher readings than any of the previous days in that cycle.

7. A woman's menstrual cycle can easily be affected by different events. If you are using a fertility awareness method, you should be aware of the events that can offset the balance.

FACTORS THAT MAY AFFECT YOUR BASAL BODY TEMPERATURE INCLUDE:

- Colds and other respiratory tract infections
- Other infections or disease
- Temporary situational factors (jetlag, 6 AM feedings, changes in diet, etc.)

- Irregular sleeping hours
- Hot or cold beverages ingested before taking your BBT
- Use of an electric blanket
- Failure to read the thermometer correctly
- Nightmares.

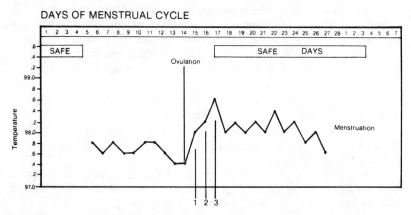

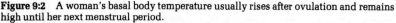

Figure 9:2 A woman's basal body temperature usually rises after ovulation and remains high until her next menstrual period.

HOW TO USE THE MUCUS METHOD

Most fertile women are able to notice fairly regular changes in the wetness just inside the vagina. These changes are caused by normal hormonal variations. You can use these changes to pinpoint the time of ovulation in each cycle. *Ovulation mucus is clear, abundant, and slippery.*

1. Check your vagina each time you use the bathroom. Put a finger inside your vagina and notice how wet it feels. You will compare the degree of wetness each day. Notice also whether you can collect any mucus on your finger, and check for stickiness and stretch. Record your findings on a special chart each day.

2. Most women find the following pattern in their mucus changes each cycle:

During menstruation, blood covers up any other sensations of wetness or mucus.

78

After your menstrual period, there may be a few days when your vagina feels moist, but not distinctly wet. There is no mucus. (Some women do not have any of these *dry* days, especially if they have very short cycles—21 days long or so.)

Next you may notice thick, cloudy, whitish or yellowish, and sticky mucus. Your vagina still does not feel distinctly wet. This phase can last for several days. Consider yourself fertile as soon as you notice any mucus at all.

As ovulation nears, mucus usually becomes more abundant. You may notice an increasingly wet sensation. Mucus becomes clear, slippery, and very stretchable. You might be able to stretch it 3 or more inches between your thumb and forefinger. Consider yourself **VERY** fertile when you have this kind of mucus.

The peak or last day of wetness and abundant, clear, slippery mucus is assumed to be about the time of ovulation.

Once clear, slippery mucus has decreased and is no longer detectable, you could have either a return of thick, cloudy, sticky mucus or no mucus at all until the time of your next menstrual period.

REMEMBER: You may need to notice your own mucus changes for several cycles before you understand your personal mucus signs clearly enough to rely on this method of birth control. Also remember, if you check your vagina several times in one day, only record your **MOST FERTILE** observation for that day.

3. Assume you are fertile as soon as you notice any wetness or mucus of any kind. You remain fertile until the fourth day after your peak day.

4. The mucus technique may not give you enough advance warning of ovulation to prevent pregnancy. For more effective protection you can avoid intercourse or use another method of birth control during the first part of your cycle until 4 days after your peak mucus days.

5. A woman's menstrual cycle can be easily affected by different events. If you are using a fertility awareness method, you should be aware of a number of variables that can offset the balance.

FACTORS WHICH MAY AFFECT YOUR MUCUS READINGS INCLUDE:
- Numerous infections of the vagina
- Use of vaginal spermicides—foams, jellies, creams, and suppositories
- Douching
- Artificial lubricants
- Medications used for infections or to provide hormones
- Sexual intercourse—semen and secretions from sexual arousal.

Figure 9:3 Cervical mucus changes during the course of a normal menstrual cycle. Use this summary to help you determine your own characteristics.

Time of Cycle	Amount	Viscosity	Color	Spinnbarkeit	Ferning
post-menstruation	moderate	thick	cloudy, yellow or white	<1"	no
nearing ovulation	increasing	somewhat thick to thin	mixed cloudy and clear	1-1½"	moderate
ovulation	maximum	very thin and slippery	clear	6-8"	well developed
post-ovulation (about 3 days)	decreasing	thin	mixed cloudy and clear	4-6"	minimal or no
nearing menstruation	minimal	thick	cloudy	<1-1½"	no

Use this summary of mucus characteristics to learn about your cycle. Amount (volume) means the woman's interpretation of what she feels with her finger inside her vagina. Viscosity means the consistency of mucus. Color can vary quite a bit, and clear mucus may be tinged with blood at the time of ovulation. Spinnbarkeit means elasticity: how much can you stretch a mucus sample before it breaks? Ferning means that a sample of mucus taken on a fertile day, smeared on a glass slide, and air-dried will reveal a microscopic pattern that looks like fern leaves. (Reprinted from *Health Education Bulletin*, July 1979, by the National Clearinghouse for Family Planning Information DHEW, Bureau of Community Health Services.) (< means less than.)

TIPS FOR SUCCESS

IF YOU WANT TO USE ONE OF THE FERTILITY AWARENESS METHODS TO AVOID UNWANTED PREGNANCIES, GO TO A FAMILY PLANNING CLINIC, A WOMAN'S HEALTH CENTER, OR TO SOME OTHER SOURCE OF COUNSELING TO OBTAIN MORE EXTENSIVE INFORMATION, FORMS ON HOW TO MONITOR THESE CYCLIC CHANGES, AND ENCOURAGEMENT.

1. COMBINING ALL THREE TECHNIQUES FOR FERTILITY AWARENESS will probably improve your effectiveness. If you record your menstrual dates, BBTs, and mucus changes you will probably be able to pinpoint your fertile days more accurately.

2. THE NUMBER OF DAYS YOU CAN HAVE INTERCOURSE WILL BE INCREASED IF you also include the first 4 days during menstruation, provided your cycles are at least 25 days long. While some couples may enjoy intercourse during menstruation, others may find it unpleasant because of the menstrual blood in the vagina. This inconvenience can be reduced by using a diaphragm during intercourse. The diaphragm will temporarily hold back menstrual blood. Couples who object to using birth control devices may accept the use of a diaphragm during menses, as it serves essentially no contraceptive function.

3. WATCH FOR ALL YOUR CYCLIC SIGNS. You may notice mid-cycle abdominal pain with ovulation, changes in your mood or sex drive, or breast changes. Use all the information you have to help identify ovulation accurately.

4. IF YOUR PATTERN IS NOT CLEAR, DO NOT GUESS. You should assume that you are fertile.

5. GIVE SERIOUS THOUGHT TO USING A BACKUP METHOD like diaphragm, condoms, foam, or spermicidal suppositories or tablets. If you do use a backup method when you are unsure about your chart signs, or have intercourse close to or during your fertile interval, you will have much more effective birth control protection.

GO BACK TO YOUR CLINICIAN

1. IF YOU MISS A MENSTRUAL PERIOD or suspect for any reason that you may be pregnant.

2. IF YOUR PATTERNS ARE NOT CLEAR or you need help interpreting your observations.

3. IF YOUR CYCLE LENGTHS VARY WIDELY or you are unable to establish a menstrual pattern. You may need to consider an alternative method of birth control.

4. FOR YOUR YEARLY GYNECOLOGICAL EXAMINATION.

CHAPTER 10:
WITHDRAWAL

If you are using the withdrawal method you may have intercourse until ejaculation is about to occur, at which point the male withdraws his penis from the vagina. Ejaculation occurs completely away from the vagina and the external genitalia of the female.

The withdrawal method does NOT require any mechanical devices, medications or chemicals, or careful calculations. And, it is available all the time at no cost.

The withdrawal method does have its disadvantages. It is NOT a highly effective way to prevent pregnancy. Pregnancy can and does often occur, especially if you fail to exercise self-control or do not wipe off the pre-ejaculatory fluid from the penis. Some preliminary ejaculatory liquid (often said to be semen stored in the prostate or urethra or the Cowper's gland) can escape before the penis is withdrawn. Because of the release of this fluid, the likelihood of failure increases if there is more than one orgasm within a short span of time. This fluid contains more sperm after a recent ejaculation.

ADDITIONAL DIFFICULTIES MAY INCLUDE:
- Failure to correctly estimate the time of ejaculation;
- Failure to suppress the natural urge to push; and
- Failure to resist the desire to complete the act of intercourse.

Some couples find withdrawal a "less loving" form of sexual intimacy. One reason for this is that withdrawal may abruptly end sexual contact.

USING THE WITHDRAWAL METHOD

1. Before intercourse, the fluid at the tip of the penis should be wiped off completely. Millions of sperm are contained in this drop of liquid.

2. When the man feels that he is about to ejaculate or reach orgasm, he should remove his penis from inside the vagina. Be sure that ejaculation takes place away from the entrance to the vagina.

3. Withdrawal is not a good birth control method if you intend to have repeated acts of intercourse.

4. Withdrawal in not a good birth control method if you have difficulty controlling ejaculation.

5. Try to have a supply of birth control foam or some type of spermicide available in case of an accident.

CHAPTER 11: ABSTINENCE

Abstinence is an alternative to sexual intercourse. Not all people want to, or even do, have sexual relations. In fact, in many areas of the world today, sexual intercourse is prohibited during certain periods of a woman's or man's life.

Abstinence involves making a conscious decision NOT to engage in sexual intercourse; it means balancing your cultural, personal, and moral values. It often demands dedication and will power.

Your decision to abstain from intercourse may be a voluntary or an involuntary decision. Your reasons may range from fear of pregnancy to simple lack of interest. Or, abstinence may result from any of the following:

- Lack of opportunity for intercourse (widowed/divorced/single)
- Periods of abstinence required by fertility awareness methods
- Sexual dysfunction
- Aging, illness, or injury.

You are the only one who can decide which is the right choice *for you and your partner*—sexual intercourse or abstinence. Although abstinence is often overlooked, REMEMBER it is (and can be for you) an acceptable and comfortable contraceptive option. If you and your partner decide to be intimate without intercourse, remember that there are other ways of being close. The next chapter discusses some of these ways.

How to Say No (see page 86) was originally written for teenagers. The advice, however, can be useful to anyone.

HOW TO SAY NO!

Sometimes you find yourself in a situation that's getting out of hand. Perhaps when you're kissing and his hands are around your shoulders and neck and then, all of a sudden, they're wandering down your body. You want to stop. You don't want things to go any farther. Well, how do you say "no" without hurting his feelings? How do you say "no" without making him stop liking you and saying bad things about you to all his friends? How do you say "no" so that he knows you mean it?

HERE ARE SOME SUGGESTIONS:

- Work out an understanding. Talk things over before you go too far.
- Remind yourself that the man doesn't have to have it; if you can wait, he can wait.
- Don't be angry. Be firm, move away, get up and do something so the mood changes.
- You don't have to explain, but you can give a reason if you want to. "I've made up my mind to wait" or "I'm not ready to get involved," or whatever answer you're comfortable with.
- Remind yourself of the responsibility of birth control and parenthood.
- Respect yourself. Know that the right person will wait for you.

HOW TO SAY NO! is part of the *It's a New Decade* series of pamphlets designed to encourage self-care thorough awareness and education. Over 50 pamphlets are available through the Emory University Family Planning Program, Publications Department, 80 Butler Street, S.E., P.O. Box 26060, Atlanta, Georgia 30303.

CHAPTER 12: SEX WITHOUT INTERCOURSE ("Outercourse")

There are many ways of expressing yourself sexually. Besides the conventional penis-in-vagina intercourse, other activities can also be intimate and sexual. These activities stretch over a broad range, from holding hands, hugging, kissing, petting, dancing to mutual masturbation, oral-genital sex, and the use of stimulating devices such as vibrators. Many of these alternate expressions, which may be more intimate than sexual intercourse, may come before, after, or in place of sexual intercourse.

Here are some instances when you might prefer "outercourse,"— other forms of sexual pleasure instead of sexual intercourse.

1. **WHEN YOUR BIRTH CONTROL METHOD IS NOT IMMEDIATELY AVAILABLE.** Sometimes you may want to engage in sexual intimacy but find that you don't have your diaphragm, condoms, or spermicide. Sex without intercourse allows you to enjoy physical closeness and sexual pleasure without the worry of an unwanted pregnancy.

2. **IF YOU OR YOUR PARTNER HAS SOME SORT OF MEDICAL CONDITION,** and you have been advised to refrain from intercourse. This is especially true if you or your partner has an infection or has just had pelvic surgery, if either of you have certain handicaps, or if you are in the late stages of pregnancy, etc.

3. **IF YOU ARE BEGINNING A NEW RELATIONSHIP,** and you want to express yourself sexually, yet not have intercourse. This time of courtship gives you an opportunity for intellectual, emotional, and physical intimacy. It is a time for mutual sharing, problem-solving, and testing. Courtship may lead to penis-in-vagina intercourse, but intercourse, although important, is only a small part of the courtship ritual. Holding and touching are even more important. They answer many human needs that are not strictly sexual. *Everybody needs to be touched regularly.*

4. **WHEN SEX THERAPY IS BEING USED TO HELP A PROBLEM.** If you have sexual problems, trying new forms of sexual stimulation can help increase your ability to achieve orgasm and to enjoy intercourse. Sex therapy is just one way of dealing with such a problem.

5. **IF YOU ARE EXPLORING NEW WAYS** to get sexual gratification.

It is important for you and your partner to develop your own style. Do not worry about what is *right* or *wrong,* for there is no right or wrong way to engage in foreplay or sexual intercourse. Do what comes naturally and what is comfortable *for you and your partner.*

CHAPTER 13:
BREAST-FEEDING

IMPORTANT THINGS TO REMEMBER

Breast-feeding may protect against pregnancy by delaying the return of ovulation (the release of an egg from the ovary) following childbirth. The suckling action can cause a temporary drop in the release of brain (pituitary gland) hormones that normally trigger release of an egg from the ovary. Although breastfeeding, or lactation, is an excellent way to feed your baby, it is NOT a highly reliable method of birth control. The reason for this is simple. Although breast-feeding may provide some protection against pregnancy, it does not postpone menstruation indefinitely; and it IS possible for a woman to get pregnant before she regains her menstrual period. There is presently NO WAY of knowing when ovulation or menstruation will resume. And your protection drops rapidly as soon as supplementary milk or food is given to the baby. This decreases the overall breast milk needed and sends a signal to the brain to start ovulation again.

A COMMON CAUSE OF ACCIDENTAL PREGNANCY

Ovulation can occur as early as 3 weeks or so following your delivery. Many women believe that lactation is foolproof and that a second pregnancy is out of the question. This is not true. Be sure to use a birth control method or abstain from intercourse if you want to avoid another pregnancy.

BREAST-FEEDING AND OTHER BIRTH CONTROL METHODS

If you are having sexual intercourse while nursing your baby, you will need an effective, yet safe, method of birth control for you to use while nursing. You may decide to switch methods once you stop breast-feeding.

Regular birth control Pills, which contain estrogen as well as progestin, tend to reduce the amount of breast milk produced. Most clinicians in the United States do not recommend Pills containing estrogen for women who are nursing. Try to find a contraceptive that contains no hormones, or use Mini-Pills, which contain only progestin and are often provided to nursing women.

Mini-Pills do not alter amount or content of breast milk. However, progestin, the hormone contained in Mini-Pills, does appear in very small quantities in breast milk. For women who want to use a hormonal method of birth control while nursing, Mini-Pills are probably the best choice.

Intrauterine devices (IUDS) may cause discomfort for some nursing women. This discomfort is a result of uterine contractions caused by infant suckling. Usually this is not much of a problem.

Fertility awareness methods may be very difficult for nursing mothers to use since their menstrual periods tend to be irregular. If preventing another pregnancy is a major concern, perhaps this method should be used with a backup method or its use delayed until it is possible to establish careful and consistent calculations of your *safe* days. Remember that the first ovulation (release of an egg) may occur BEFORE the first menstrual period.

Diaphragms, vaginal spermicides, foam, and condoms do not affect your breast milk production and have no known harmful effects on your infant. You may find that using contraceptive foam or lubricants, such as KY Jelly, H-R Lubricating Jelly, or saliva is helpful for intercourse. After childbirth and during breast-feeding, you will have a normal drop in hormone production. This causes a drop in normal vaginal lubrication.

If you are planning to have a *sterilization* performed postpartum (immediately after delivery), it may be desirable to avoid heavy sedation or general anesthesia sometimes used for this surgery. These medications can affect your infant via breast-feeding. It may instead be possible to have local anesthesia or a method like spinal anesthesia for your surgery.

Breast-feeding's contraceptive protection diminishes the longer you nurse your child and the more you supplement breast-feeding with food or bottled milk. This occurs because you will tend to ovulate sooner if you supplement breast-feeding.

TIPS FOR BREAST-FEEDING

1. USE A METHOD OF BIRTH CONTROL whenever you have intercourse. Breast-feeding is not a reliable method of contraception.

2. BREAST-FEEDING IS A CONVENIENT, INEXPENSIVE AND NUTRITIOUS WAY to feed your baby.

3. MENSTRUAL BLEEDING DOES NOT AFFECT THE QUALITY NOR THE QUANTITY OF YOUR BREAST MILK. Menstruation should not be a reason to stop breast-feeding.

4. WHILE NURSING YOUR CHILD. YOUR OWN NUTRITION IS VERY IMPORTANT. You have greater nutritional requirements, which can be satisfied, for the most part, by a glass of milk and a peanut buter sandwich. There are other sources of calcium such as cheese, yogurt, and custard, if you do not tolerate milk.

5. NURSING WOMEN WHO SMOKE MAY TRANSFER NICOTINE TO THEIR INFANT through their breast milk, which can harm the baby. Similarly, it is not advisable for infants to inhale smoke. Try very hard to stop smoking.

6. WE DO NOT KNOW ALL THERE IS TO KNOW ABOUT THE EFFECT HORMONES IN THE MILK HAVE ON BABIES. Both estrogens and progestins from hormone contraceptives do appear in small amounts in breast milk. Information is not yet available to show what immediate or long-term effects, if any, are caused by exposure to contraceptive hormones during infancy.

The use of an estrogen (and possibly of a progestin) may interfere with initiation of lactation and may diminish the amount and duration of milk flow.

**WHEN IT COMES TO FEEDING YOUR CHILD,
BREAST IS BEST!**

GO BACK TO YOUR CLINICIAN

1. If you suspect for any reason that you may be pregnant again.

2. If you have fever, abnormal breast tenderness or discharge, or you believe your flow of breast milk is inadequate.

3. For your 6 weeks postpartum examination.

CHAPTER 14:
MORNING-AFTER BIRTH
CONTROL/EMERGENCY
BIRTH CONTROL

Almost anyone can have a birth control emergency. Some common situations, when you might want to consider emergency birth control or morning-after treatment, include the following.

1. You had intercourse when you hadn't planned to—and did not use any birth control.

2. You were using fertility awareness methods and realized during or after intercourse that you had miscalculated your fertile days.

3. Your partner was using a condom and it broke or slipped off, spilling sperm in or near the vagina.

4. You were using a vaginal foaming tablet and realized after intercourse that it had not dissolved.

5. You were using a diaphragm and realized after intercourse that it was not in proper position.

6. You and your partner were planning to use withdrawal but he ejaculated before he had time to withdraw.

7. You had intercourse "just this once" without using your regular birth control method.

IMMEDIATE EMERGENCY OPTIONS

If you realize during or immediately after intercourse that you were not protected, then you can try the following steps. These steps are not foolproof, and you should see your doctor as soon as it is reasonable.

1. **INSERT AN APPLICATOR FULL OF SPERMICIDAL FOAM,** jelly, or cream into your vagina right away.

2. **IF YOU DON'T HAVE A SPERMICIDE ON HAND,** then you can try a warm water douche to thoroughly rinse the vagina. Douche as soon after intercourse as possible (run, don't walk). This option is probably not as effective as using spermicide, but it may decrease the likelihood of conception.

MORNING-AFTER OPTIONS

Morning-after birth control treatment does not make sense if you have had unprotected intercourse several times during your cycle. You may already have conceived, so that treatment with an IUD or with hormones would not work and might be dangerous for you or might adversely affect the pregnancy. Before recommending treatment, your clinician will carefully review the dates you have had intercourse and confirm that you are not already pregnant. If you or your clinician cannot be sure, then your best option may be to wait and see.

Your treatment alternatives may include:

1. JUST WAIT AND SEE. The overall chance of getting pregnant if you have had unprotected intercourse just once during a cycle is only about 2% (2 in 100). Even if that one intercourse is during your most fertile 24 hours, your chance is probably no greater than 30% (30 in 100).

If your next period is on time, you can breathe a sigh of relief, but be sure your birth control needs are covered from then on. If your period is late, have a pregnancy test and see your clinician. You may decide to continue the pregnancy or have an early abortion, if you are pregnant.

2. HAVE AN IUD INSERTED WITHIN 5 DAYS. A copper IUD prevents implantation and growth of the fertilized egg if it is inserted within 5 days after unprotected intercourse. This morning-after approach makes most sense if you have been planning on using an IUD anyway. Read the chapter on the IUD in this book, and be sure to discuss any questions you have with your clinician.

3. CONSIDER MORNING-AFTER HORMONE TREATMENT. A short hormone treatment begun within 24 to 72 hours after unprotected intercourse can stop conception and/or implantation. Research first tested and used DES (diethylstibestrol); newer studies, however, have found success using ordinary OVRAL birth control Pills which have a lower hormone dose. If you don't have OVRAL Pills on hand, you will need to see your clinician as soon as possible. The treatment is most effective if it is started within 24 hours.

Before you take morning-after hormone treatment, read the chapter on birth control Pills in this book. Be sure to review the list of questions at the beginning of the chapter and discuss any YES answers with your clinician.

USING MORNING-AFTER HORMONE TREATMENT

1. **TAKE 2 OVRAL PILLS IMMEDIATELY** (within 24 to 72 hours after intercourse). **THEN TAKE 2 MORE OVRAL PILLS** twelve (12) hours after your first dose of Pills.

2. **YOU MAY HAVE NAUSEA** from the Pills. It is usually mild and stops within a day or so after treatment. If you vomit within an hour after taking your 2 Pills, call your clinician. You may need to take additional Pills to make up for the ones lost in vomiting, and your clinician may prescribe anti-nausea medication.

3. **YOUR NEXT MENSTRUAL PERIOD SHOULD BEGIN SOMETIME WITHIN THE NEXT 2 TO 3 WEEKS.** If your period has not started in 3 weeks, see your clinician for an exam and pregnancy test.

4. **WATCH FOR PILL DANGER SIGNS:**
   - SEVERE HEADACHES
   - BLURRED VISION
   - CHEST PAIN
   - ABDOMINAL PAIN
   - LEG PAIN

Complications are not likely to occur with the short morning-after treatment, but if you have any of the danger signs, you should see your clinician right away or go to an emergency room.

5. **IMMEDIATELY START USING A BIRTH CONTROL METHOD.** Morning-after treatment is meant for one-time protection only. Use condoms, foam, spermicide tablets, or your diaphragm until your next period. After your period, you can start taking Pills or Mini-Pills, if you wish, or continue with your condoms, foam, or diaphragm.

CHAPTER 15: WHAT IF YOUR METHOD FAILS?

If you are using an effective birth control method carefully and consistently, it is quite unlikely that you will become pregnant. If you do conceive while you are using one of the methods, however, you may want to consider the possible effects the method might have on your pregnancy or fetus. This is not so important if you are sure you would have an abortion. If you feel you might continue the pregnancy, then you will probably want to consider this factor in choosing your method of birth control.

Abstinence: No harmful effects are known unless the accidental pregnancy was conceived very early or very late in the woman's fertile interval. In that case, risks would be the same as for fertility awareness.

Withdrawal: No harmful effects are known.

Fertility Awareness Methods (rhythm, periodic abstinence, natural family planning): Some researchers have linked this method with higher rates of fetal abnormalities and spontaneous abortion. Accidental pregnancies that occur when couples are practicing fertility awareness are likely to have been conceived either very early or very late in the woman's monthly fertile interval. Researchers believe that this increases the likelihood that an old egg (aged egg) or old sperm (aged sperm) will begin the pregnancy. Old eggs and old sperm are known to be a cause of chromosome (gene) problems and other fetal abnormalities.

Regular Birth Control Pills: Studies of pregnancy conceived while a woman is taking Pills have shown slightly higher-than-normal rates of spontaneous abortion and of fetal abnormalities. The overall risk, however, is not very high. Researchers estimate that about 1 fetus in every 1,000 exposed to contraceptive hormones might have an abnormality caused by the Pill. Other researchers estimate an even lower rate of abnormalities caused by Pills—2 fetuses in every 10,000 exposed to Pills. The chance that the pregnancy may be an ectopic (tubal) pregnancy is higher for women taking Pills than for those who don't.

Mini-Pills: No studies of pregnancy problems among Mini-Pill users have been reported. However, since Mini-Pills contain a low dose of progestin (similar to the progestin in combined birth control Pills), there may be some increase in risks.

Intrauterine Device: The risk of spontaneous abortion (miscarriage) is very high when pregnancy is conceived with an IUD in place. If the IUD remains in place, the risk of having spontaneous abortion is 50%. If the IUD is removed early in pregnancy, the risk is lower, about 25%. Also, the woman's risk for serious uterine infection is high. And the chance that the pregnancy may be an ectopic (tubal or ovarian) pregnancy is higher when conception occurs with an IUD than it would be if the woman were using a diaphragm, spermicide, condom, or no birth control. There are no well-documented problems as to the occurrence of fetal abnormalities.

Diaphragm, Foam, Jelly, Cream, Suppositories, Tablets: These methods are grouped together because chemical spermicides are in all of them. A recent study has found that pregnancy conceived among women who were spermicide users may have a higher overall risk of fetal abnormality. Further research will be required in order to find out how and when spermicide exposure causes this problem and to be sure it really is a problem. Overall, only about 1 fetus in every 1,000 possibly exposed to spermicides might have an abnormality linked to spermicides.

Condoms: No harmful effects are known.

Tubal Sterilization: There is a much higher risk that the pregnancy will not be in the uterus, but in the fallopian tube (ectopic pregnancy), should the pregnancy occur following a tubal ligation.

CHAPTER 16: ABORTION

BEFORE YOU HAVE AN ABORTION, think about the following questions. If you have any **YES** answers, be sure to discuss them with your clinician.

YES/NO   Am I uncomfortable with the idea of having an abortion?

YES/NO   Does having an abortion go against my religious or ethical values?

YES/NO   Have I had confirmation of a pregnancy?

YES/NO   Will I have trouble getting in touch with my doctor if I have complications after my abortion?

IMPORTANT THINGS TO REMEMBER

1. **INDUCED ABORTION IS A LEGAL PROCEDURE** in the United States. New federal regulations have, however, prohibited the use of federal funds for abortion except in the case of rape or incest, or when pregnancy endangers a woman's life. However, unless the Supreme Court reverses its 1973 position or an amendment to the Constitution is passed, abortion will remain legal throughout the United States. Approximately 1.3 million women choose to have pregnancy termination procedures in the United States each year.

2. **ABORTION IS SAFEST EARLY IN PREGNANCY.** Keep track of your menstrual cycle and be aware of pregnancy signs (breast tenderness, nausea, frequent urination, etc.). If you believe you are pregnant, get a pregnancy test immediately. Do **NOT** wait! A delay in having a pregnancy test is the major difference for women who receive the safer first trimester abortions or women who receive second trimester abortions.

3. **IF YOUR PREGNANCY TEST IS POSITIVE,** explore your feelings about the pregnancy. There are many professionals (counselors, family planners, doctors, nurses, and clinicians) with whom you can speak about financial assistance, further counseling, contraceptive services, abortion services, prenatal services, and male/female sterilization services.

4. **CHOOSING TO HAVE AN ABORTION SHOULD BE COMPLETELY VOLUNTARY.** *You are the only one who can make the decision;* no one should make that decision for you!

5. **THE RISK OF DYING OR DEVELOPING A COMPLICATION** from an abortion is slight. Since abortions became legal, deaths due to abortions have

decreased significantly. Today, in fact, carrying a pregnancy to term is riskier than having an early abortion. The risk of dying from a full-term pregnancy is about 25 times greater in the United States than the risk of dying from an abortion during the first eight weeks of pregnancy.

HAVING YOUR ABORTION

Before an abortion can be performed your clinician will review your medical history, examine you, and conduct some laboratory tests.

The abortion procedure removes the entire products of conception, including the placenta, fetal parts, and some of the uterine tissue. Abortions are performed with a number of different surgical and medical methods. The surgical methods used for early abortions (first trimester) include vacuum curettage, dilation and curettage (D & C), dilation and evacuation (D & E), hysterotomy, and rarely, hysterectomy. The medical methods used for late (2nd trimester) abortions include putting prostaglandins, saline, or urea into the amniotic sac. These medical alternatives cause a woman to go into labor and to deliver the fetus and placenta.

Try to arrange for your partner or a friend to accompany you when you have your abortion. If you have cramps or feel shaky or weak afterward, you will be glad to have company for your trip home.

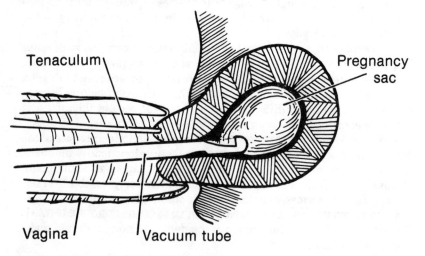

Figure 16:1   The vacuum tube draws the pregnancy sac out of the uterus at the time of an abortion.

If you are allergic to any drugs or to general anesthesia, TELL your doctor BEFORE he or she performs the abortion. This is extremely important to your health.

MINIMIZING YOUR RISKS

Complications will be lowest if:
1. Your general health is good;
2. The pregnancy is diagnosed early, and the abortion occurs early;
3. The abortion is performed using sterile surgical (vacuum) techniques;
4. The clinician is well-trained and experienced;
5. You learn the danger signs to watch for after an abortion;
6. Follow-up care is available on a 24-hour basis if problems arise after abortion;
7. The tissue removed is examined carefully so that the possibility of incomplete abortion, ectopic pregnancy, or molar pregnancy can be recognized at the time of surgery;
8. You do not have gonorrhea;
9. Rh immune globulin is given to you if you are a Rh negative woman.

WHAT TO DO AFTER YOUR ABORTION

When your surgery is over, you may eat or drink anything you like or return to your normal activities. Most women find it best to avoid especially strenuous exercise for the next few days. Be guided by how you feel. It is important that you read these instructions carefully and follow them closely. Do NOT hesitate to call your doctor or clinic if you have a problem or question.

The amount of bleeding and cramping that may follow varies from woman to woman. Some women have none at all, but most have cramps and bleeding during the first 2 weeks after an abortion. If for 2 days in a row you experience bleeding that is heavier than the heaviest day of your normal menstrual period, you should call your doctor or clinic. It is not unusual for light bleeding (spotting) to occur for as long as 4 weeks after an abortion. Your next normal period should begin in 4 to 6 weeks. (If you are taking birth control Pills, your period probably will come after you finish your first Pill pack.)

To help decrease your risk of infection, do NOT put anything in your vagina for the first week after your abortion.

- Do not use tampons—use sanitary pads only.
- Do not have intercourse.
- Do not douche.

For a week, take your temperature carefully each day at noon and before going to sleep. Call your doctor or clinic if your temperature reaches 100°F.

If you are taking Tylenol or aspirin for pain, take your temperature before taking the medication.

Be sure to have a follow-up examination within 2 or 3 weeks after the procedure.

PROBLEMS TO WATCH FOR

Infections, retained products of conception, continued pregnancy, cervical or uterine trauma, and bleeding are all potential, short-term, post-abortion complications. Should any of these complications occur, your body will alert you to them by sending off signs. Watch for these danger signs and get help *immediately* if any develop following the abortion.

CALL FOR HELP

The words **CALL FOR HELP** provide a good reminder to the person who has just had an abortion and wants to know what to watch out for right after the abortion.

C: Cramps or pain.
F: Fever.
H: Hemorrhage.

Be sure to **CALL FOR HELP** if any of these problems arise!

GO BACK TO YOUR CLINICIAN OR GO TO AN EMERGENCY ROOM

If you notice any of the following:
- **FEVER** (temperature of 100.4°F or more), chills, or malaise (fatigue, aching).

- **CRAMPING** or abdominal pain that is severe or persistent.
- **ABDOMINAL TENDERNESS**, pain with pressure, movement, or cough.
- **BLEEDING** that is heavy or prolonged.
- **ABNORMAL VAGINAL DISCHARGE** or foul smelling discharge.
- **ALLERGY SYMPTOMS** like a rash, hives, asthma, or difficulty in breathing.
- **PREGNANCY SYMPTOMS** that persist, or a delay in your first menstrual period.

TIPS FOR SUCCESS

1. **CHOOSE A CLINICIAN WHO IS EXPERIENCED IN PERFORMING ABORTIONS.** This will help you have a safe abortion with the least risks. You can call Planned Parenthood or your local health department for information and referrals.

2. **AFTER THE ABORTION, USE BIRTH CONTROL** when you have sexual intercourse. Your doctor or counselor will explain your birth control options and help you find a method that suits your needs. Read Chapter 1 in this book for information on choosing a birth control method.

3. **MAKE YOUR HEALTH YOUR FIRST PRIORITY.** See your clinician right away if you have any of the danger signs, even in your symptoms are only mild ones.

CHAPTER 17:
STERILIZATION

BEFORE YOU HAVE STERILIZATION SURGERY, think about the following questions. If you have YES answers, be sure to discuss them with your clinician.

YES/NO   Do I want any more children?

YES/NO   Does my spouse want any more children?

YES/NO   If I were to remarry or my spouse were to die, would it be possible that I might want children then?

YES/NO   Is there any chance I might be pregnant right now?

YES/NO   Have I had a recent infection?

YES/NO   Do I have any fears that sterilization will have any effect upon my ability to function sexually?

IMPORTANT THINGS TO REMEMBER

1. STERILIZATION GENERALLY SHOULD BE CONSIDERED A PERMANENT and IRREVERSIBLE method of contraception. Surgery to reverse sterilization (rejoin the tubes) is possible in some cases, but it is not always successful, and it is difficult and costly. If there is any chance that you may want children in the future, you should delay having a sterilization operation.

2. IF A COUPLE IS CONSIDERING A STERILIZATION PROCEDURE AND ALL FACTORS ARE EQUAL, THEN VASECTOMY MAY MAKE MORE SENSE. Vasectomy is a safer and easier procedure. The complication rate and the cost of vasectomy are lower than are the complication rate and the cost for tubal ligation.

3. STERILIZATION OPERATIONS SHOULD NOT ALTER SEX DRIVE, SEXUAL COMPETENCE, OR SEXUAL ENJOYMENT. Vasectomy will not affect a man's ability to have an erection or to ejaculate. Similarly, tubal ligation should not influence a woman's sex drive or menstrual cycle.

4. NO STATE OR HOSPITAL CAN REQUIRE THAT YOU BE A CERTAIN AGE, be married, or have a certain number of children before you can have a sterilization operation. The decision is up to you and your clinician.

5. INFORMED CONSENT IS IMPORTANT before you agree to have a sterilization. The decision MUST be completely voluntary. If you are consider-

ing sterilization, you should be well-informed about the procedure and its effects.

COMMON CAUSES OF ACCIDENTAL PREGNANCY

1. THE WOMAN WAS ALREADY PREGNANT at the time the tubal ligation was performed. To prevent this, schedule your sterilization operation during or just after your menstrual period.

2. THE MAN DID NOT HAVE 2 NEGATIVE SPERM COUNTS before he had sexual intercourse without birth control. Be sure to use a backup method of birth control until your negative sperm count has been confirmed. Unfortunately, there is no way a woman can check to be sure she is sterile after a tubal ligation.

3. THE MAN'S VAS DEFERENS (TUBES) OR THE WOMAN'S FALLOPIAN TUBES GREW BACK TOGETHER. In a small percentage of cases the ends of the tubes will rejoin, and the surgery will have to be repeated. Although this is a very rare occurrence, it has been known to happen.

STERILIZATION FOR MEN: VASECTOMY

Vasectomy, the sterilization operation for men, is a surgical procedure that cuts and closes the vas deferens located in each testicle. By cutting the vas, sperm are prevented from combining with ejaculatory fluid and from entering the woman's vagina (see diagram on page 104).

WHAT TO DO BEFORE YOUR VASECTOMY

1. ON THE AFTERNOON OF YOUR SCHEDULED SURGERY, with a pair of scissors cut the hair from the scrotum and from around the penis to approximately ¼ inch in length.

2. SHOWER OR BATHE, washing the penis and scrotum thoroughly to remove all loose hairs.

3. HAVE SOMEONE ACCOMPANY YOU when you are going to have the operation. Do not plan on driving home yourself.

4. PLAN TO REMAIN QUIET FOR ABOUT 48 HOURS following the vasectomy.

5. BE PREPARED FOR SOME PAIN AND SWELLING in the scrotal region following the vasectomy. The scrotum may be somewhat black and blue,

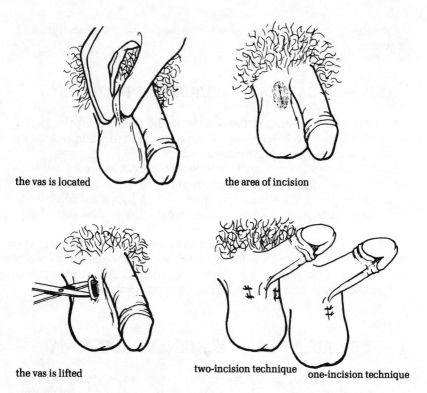

the vas is located

the area of incision

the vas is lifted

two-incision technique

one-incision technique

Figure 17:1 Vasectomy is a fairly safe and easy medical procedure.

and there may be a small amount of bleeding. Ice packs, rest, and time all decrease these problems.

6. **IT IS VERY IMPORTANT FOR YOU TO BE COMFORTABLE WITH YOUR DECI-SION** to have a vasectomy. You and your partner must be certain that you understand (and desire) this permanent operation. You can change your mind about the procedure at any time prior to the operaton.

WHAT TO DO AFTER YOUR VASECTOMY

1. **FOLLOWING THE PROCEDURE,** you should return home and rest for aproximately 48 hours. Do not shower or bathe for the first 2 days following the vasectomy. You may be able to resume your normal activities in 2 or 3 days. If possible, you should keep an ice pack on the scrotum for at

least 4 hours. This will reduce chances of swelling, bleeding, and discomfort. You may use a scrotal support for as long as you feel more comfortable with it.

2. AVOID STRENUOUS PHYSICAL EXERCISE FOR A WEEK. Strenuous exercise means hard physical exertion that you do not normally do, or lifting or straining that could bring pressure to the groin or scrotum.

3. YOU MAY START HAVING SEXUAL INTERCOURSE AFTER 2–3 DAYS if you feel that it would be comfortable (stop if it is NOT comfortable).

4. YOUR SURGEON WILL TELL YOU WHEN TO RETURN to have your stitches removed. Many surgeons use dissolving stitches which do not have to be removed.

5. REMEMBER, YOU ARE NOT STERILE IMMEDIATELY. Active sperm remain in the tubes for some time after vasectomy, so take birth control precautions until you have 2 negative sperm counts. Have a sperm count 8 weeks after your vasectomy IF there has been at least 10 ejaculations during those 8 weeks. If not, you should probably delay this test until there have been 10 ejaculations. Ejaculate (by masturbation or withdrawal) into a small, dry, wide-mouthed jar, and take it to the laboratory or to your surgeon. Repeat this 4 weeks after the first test. You may consider yourself sterile after 2 negative sperm counts.

6. ABOUT 48 HOURS FOLLOWING THE VASECTOMY, begin taking sitz baths by filling the bathtub with plain warm water and sitting in it for approximately 20 minutes. Try to do this 4 times daily, as it will help in the healing process.

7. MOST SURGEONS RECOMMEND A POST-OPERATIVE CHECKUP about a week after the operation. The doctor or nurse will simply check the incision area to see that it is healing properly.

8. AFTER SURGERY, you will probably have some pain and swelling in the scrotal region; the scrotum may be somewhat black and blue (from a small amount of bleeding.) This is normal and should not worry you. Any increase in the size of your scrotum means that you should visit or call your doctor immediately.

9. IN A SMALL PERCENTAGE OF CASES (perhaps 1 in 1,000), the ends of the vas will grow back together, and the surgery will have to be repeated. For this reason, some vasectomized men have their semen checked for sperm every 2 to 4 years.

10. WATCH FOR THE FOLLOWING DANGER SIGNALS and notify your doctor if any occur:
- FEVER (over 100.4°F)
- BLEEDING (from the site of the incision)
- EXCESSIVE PAIN
- SWELLING (of the scrotum)

DOES VASECTOMY CAUSE ATHEROSCLEROSIS?

Lately, public attention has focused on the possible link between vasectomy and atherosclerosis. Atherosclerosis is a condition of the cardiovascular system that can often lead to heart disease, peripheral vascular disease, and stroke. Two recent studies performed on small numbers of monkeys have shown that there is an increase in atherosclerosis in those monkeys who had had vasectomies.

Are these findings applicable to men? To date, large studies on vasectomized humans have not confirmed the atherosclerotic changes seen in vasectomized monkeys. This is encouraging; but researchers admit that the data from the monkey studies are still disturbing—disturbing enough to warrant several investigations of vasectomized men.

It is important to note, however, that many factors such as diet, smoking, obesity, and heredity are known to play a significant role in the development of atherosclerosis.

What should you do with this information? If you are planning on having a vasectomy and have no reservations, especially in regard to the above information, then proceed as normal. If you have some concerns about this subject, or if you are considered a "high risk" patient, then you might prefer to delay the operation until more evidence is in. We recommend that you discuss this subject with your doctor before you make a decision.

STERILIZATION FOR WOMEN

There are several sterilization operations available to women. These include several tubal ligation procedures (interrupting the path of the egg by cutting, tying, or sealing shut the fallopian tubes) and hysterectomy (the removal of the uterus).

The following 2 sections detail instructions for women who choose to have a laparoscopic tubal ligation. **Remember,** there are other sterilization procedures. You and your clinician should decide on the technique which is safest *for you*. If you decide not to have a laparoscopic tubal ligation, you and your clinician will need to alter these instructions to fit your procedure.

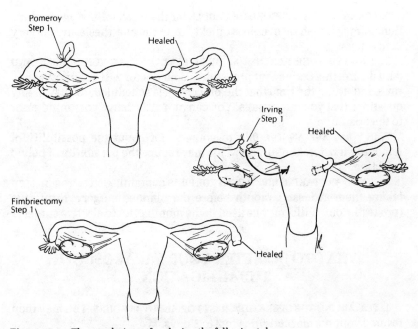

Figure 17:2 Three techniques for closing the fallopian tubes.
(Reprinted from *My Body, My Health*, John Wiley & Sons, Inc.)

WHAT TO DO BEFORE YOUR LAPAROSCOPIC TUBAL LIGATION

1. **SHOWER OR BATHE** just before coming for your surgery. Pay particular attention to washing the area around and in the umbilicus (belly button).

2. **HAVE SOMEONE ACCOMPANY YOU** to your surgery. Do not plan to drive home alone.

3. **PLAN TO REST FOR AT LEAST 48 HOURS** following the operation. Do not lift anything heavy for a week.

4. **BE PREPARED FOR:**
   - Wound pain—usually not severe and usually relieved by aspirin;
   - Shoulder and chest pain—usually causes the most discomfort of all the side effects but lasts only 24 to 48 hours. Caused by the anesthesia and by gas in the abdomen;
   - Occasional pelvic ache or discomfort.

5. **PLAN TO HAVE A FLEXIBLE SCHEDULE** for the week following sterilization. Some women recover less quickly from the anesthesia and surgery than others.

6. **YOU AND YOUR PARTNER MUST BE CERTAIN THAT YOU UNDERSTAND** (and desire) this permanent procedure. Your doctor will be happy, at any time, including the time that the procedure is scheduled, to answer any questions that you might have. You can **ALWAYS** change your mind prior to the operation.

7. **IF YOU HAVE AN IUD**, talk to your doctor about the possibility of removing it before the surgery. This may reduce the possibility of pelvic infection.

8. **IF YOU ARE TAKING BIRTH CONTROL PILLS** containing an estrogen, stop taking them at least 1 month before the planned surgery. Mini-Pills (progestin-only Pills) may be used in the month prior to elective surgery.

WHAT TO DO AFTER YOUR LAPAROSCOPIC TUBAL LIGATION

1. **FOLLOWING THE OPERATION, REST FOR ABOUT 48 HOURS.** You may then resume your normal activities in 2 to 3 days.

2. **AVOID INTERCOURSE FOR 1 WEEK.** After that, you may have intercourse when it is comfortable to do so.

3. **AVOID STRENUOUS LIFTING** for about a week to allow the abdominal incisions time to heal.

4. **CALL YOUR PHYSICIAN PROMPTLY IF YOU DEVELOP:**
   ● FEVER greater than 100°F;
   ● FAINTING SPELLS;
   ● ABDOMINAL PAIN that is persistent or increasing; or
   ● BLEEDING from wounds.

5. **YOU MAY TAKE ASPIRIN IF YOU DEVELOP MINOR PAINS.** If this is not enough to control the pain, call your doctor.

6. **RETURN TO YOUR DOCTOR** or clinic in a month after the procedure to make sure that the wound is healing well.

7. **STERILIZATION PROVIDES IMMEDIATE PROTECTION** against pregnancy, providing you did not ovulate during the 48 hours before the surgery. You need not use any method of contraception.

REMEMBER that sterilization procedures are not 100% effective. If you should miss a period or think you are pregnant, you should see your clinician for an exam and pregnancy test as soon as possible.

CHAPTER 18: SEXUALLY TRANSMISSIBLE INFECTIONS

GENERAL INFORMATION ABOUT SEXUALLY TRANSMISSIBLE INFECTIONS

Gynecological infections are quite common today. They affect men and women, the rich and the poor, the individual with one sexual partner, and the individual with many sexual partners. They affect all races, all ethnic groups, and individuals with a variety of sexual patterns. Sexually transmissible infections include so many more infections than just gonorrhea and syphilis. Most people who have sexual intercourse for a number of years will develop one or more of the infections described in this chapter.

If you suspect that you have caught or developed an infection, contact your doctor or clinic. Most infections need treatment, for without treatment, serious medical complications can arise.

You should know, however, that a vaginal discharge does not always mean you have an infection. A clear or cloudy discharge with little or no odor is completely normal. The amount of normal discharge varies for each woman. The mucus given off by the vagina and cervix is the body's natural way of cleaning itself. If the discharge has an unpleasant odor, changes color, or causes itching or swelling, you should have an examination by your clinician, because you may have an infection.

Listed on page 111 are 11 infections that are fairly common in the United States. These infections, which affect the reproductive tract and the urinary tract, are by no means a total listing. For more information about other infections we suggest you consult a local gynecological textbook or your doctor.

SOME POINTS TO CONSIDER ABOUT SEXUALLY TRANSMISSIBLE INFECTIONS

1. YOU SHOULD NOT HAVE SEXUAL INTERCOURSE until your infection is cured. If, however, you do have intercourse, make use of condoms; they will provide some protection for your partner. Consider the use of condoms for several weeks, even if your infection seems to be cured.

2. YOU SHOULD CONTINUE TAKING MEDICATIONS throughout the prescribed course of treatment, even if your symptoms subside or if your menstrual period begins.

3. OFTEN WOMEN AND MEN WITH ONE SEXUALLY TRANSMISSIBLE INFECTION HAVE A SECOND INFECTION.

4. LONG-TERM USE OF BROAD-SPECTRUM ANTIBIOTICS ampicillin, tetracycline, and metronidozole (*Flagyl*) often increases a woman's chance of getting a yeast infection (monilia).

5. AVOID IRON, MILK, AND MILK PRODUCTS for 2 hours before and 2 hours after taking tetracycline.

6. VENEREAL DISEASE AND V.D. ARE TROUBLESOME TERMS. Try to avoid using them. *Sexually transmissible infections* is a more appropriate and less value-laden phrase.

7. AVOID HAVING SEXUAL INTERCOURSE with partners you suspect have an infection.

8. TREATMENT OF BOTH PARTNERS IS NECESSARY if there is a recurrence. Treatment should usually start when the infection is diagnosed.

9. FLAGYL MUST NOT BE USED IN THE FIRST TRIMESTER of pregnancy but probably can be used in the last 2 trimesters.

10. FLAGYL IS SECRETED IN BREAST MILK. Do not breast-feed when you are being treated with *Flagyl*.

11. DO NOT DRINK ALCOHOL DURING TREATMENT WITH FLAGYL, because it produces unpleasant reactions. Wait for 12 hours after treatment before drinking alcohol.

12. SOME INFECTIONS MAY CAUSE SLIGHTLY ABNORMAL PAP SMEAR READINGS. If you had an abnormal inflammatory PAP smear result, recheck the PAP smear 3-6 months after treatment, when your infection has ended.

A chart has been developed to help you better understand 11 infections. For each disease we have listed its symptoms, potential medical complications, treatment, the necessity of treating the partner, special instructions, and preventive measures.

TABLE 18.1 Sexually Transmissible Infections

NAME	SYMPTOMS (Sx)	POTENTIAL COMPLICATIONS	USUAL TREATMENT (Rx)	TREATMENT OF PARTNER	SPECIAL INSTRUCTIONS	PREVENTIVE MEASURES
CHLAMYDIA (Chlamydia trachomatis)	Burning on urination Vaginal discharge Symptoms of PID	Inflammation of the urethra, cervix, fallopian tubes Pneumonia of new-borns	Tetracycline 25 mg 4 times a day for 14-21 days. Erythromycin Sulfisoxazole	Essential	Follow instructions for cystitis, PID, or vaginitis	Avoid multiple partners
BACTERIAL VAGINITIS (Nonspecific vaginitis, Hemophilus vaginalis, Gardenerella vaginalis)	Yellow, green discharge (chalky white) Pain on urination Vaginal itching and/or painful intercourse Foul odor from discharge		Oral Flagyl 500 mg 2 times a day for 7 days, both partners Ampicillin 500 mg 4 times a day for 7-10 days, both partners	When needed	Use condoms for length of treatment	Avoid multiple partners
CYSTITIS (Bladder infection, honeymoon cystitis)	Pain or burning urination Frequent urination (small amounts) Foul-smelling, cloudy urine Lower abdominal pain Blood in urine Pain during intercourse	Bladder complications Recurrence	2 gm sulfisoxazole orally, then 1 gm 4 times a day for 10-14 days. (Some clinicians provide very short-term, high dose treatment for cystitis.) Pyridium 100 3 times a day, 24-48 hours for burning or pain. Cranberry juice to acidify the urine	When needed	Drink 10 glasses of water a day for length of treatment Use condoms, lubricated Return for follow-up urinalysis 3 to 4 weeks after treatment	Urinate often Wear cotton underpants Good hygiene is essential Drink cranberry juice Void after intercourse

111

TABLE 18.1 Sexually Transmissible Infections (Cont'd)

NAME	SYMPTOMS (Sx)	POTENTIAL COMPLICATIONS	USUAL TREATMENT (Rx)	TREATMENT OF PARTNER	SPECIAL INSTRUCTIONS	PREVENTIVE MEASURES
GONORRHEA (The Clap, the Drip, Neisseria gonorrhea)	May be asymptomatic Vaginal/Penile discharge or pain Male—Painful urination Tenderness in lymph nodes Testicular/abdominal pain Fever Female—Irregular/painful menses Painful intercourse Post-coital bleeding	Sterility Blindness Eye infections in newborns PID Arthritis	Oral treatment—3.5 gm of ampicillin or 3.0 gm of amoxicillin with 1 gm probenecid at the same time the ampicillin or amoxicillin is taken	Essential	Avoid intercourse or use condoms Refrain from oral-genital sex	Avoid multiple partners Spermicides may provide some protection Use condoms
HERPES GENITALIS	Multiple blister-like vulvar, cervical, penile sores Painful intercourse Itching of vulva and perineum Painful urination	Nervous system damage in newborns Recurrent infections in men or women Perhaps some role in development of cervical cancer	No specific treatment Analgesics (pain-relieving medicine) used locally	There is no known effective treatment	Cleanliness is essential Wear loose underwear Avoid intercourse or use condoms Use condoms for at least 6 weeks Report herpes to OB-GYN if known to be pregnant	Have a Pap smear yearly There is NO known cure Avoid intercourse, if man or woman has active infection
MONILIA (Candida albicans, yeast infection)	Thick, cottage-cheese discharge Itching/redness of external genitalia	Recurrence	Wash vagina, sponge with Betadine Mycostatin/Nystatin suppository 1 or 2 times a day for 15 days	When needed, usually not required	Wear cotton underwear Avoid tight clothing Rx may be necessary for 2 cycles	Betadine or vinegar douches Diabetes test may be needed Lose weight if overweight

112

	Symptoms	Complications	Treatment		Prevention
PELVIC INFLAMMATORY DISEASE (PID, salpingitis, endometritis)	Abdominal, back, pelvic, leg pain Fever or chills, vomiting Heavy menstrual bleeding Bleeding after intercourse Painful urination Painful intercourse	Infection Ectopic pregnancy Infertility Persistent pain	*Outpatients* — Tetracycline 500 mg orally 4 times a day for 10 days Aqueous procaine penicillin G 4.8 million units intra-muscular with 1 g probenecid Ampicillin or amoxicillin 500 mg orally 4 times a day for 10 days Flagyl 250 mg orally 4 times a day for 10 days *Hospitalized Patients*—High dose of antibiotics intreavenously, followed by oral antibiotics for 10 days	When needed	Use condoms during and after treatment **BED REST** is essential until abdominal pain subsides Abstinence for one week Watch for monilia flareups Avoid multiple partners Use condoms Avoid IUDs
PUBIC LICE (Crabs, Phthirus pubis)	Itching Lice present in pubic hair	None	Wash with Kwell shampoo, leave on area for 4 minutes May need to repeat the shampoo	If infected, must treat	Remove all visible signs of lice Wash with soap and water Massage lotion and leave for 3 hours Boil clothing and linen Avoid intercourse Good hygiene is essential

113

TABLE 18.1 Sexually Transmissible Infections (Cont'd)

NAME	SYMPTOMS (Sx)	POTENTIAL COMPLICATIONS	USUAL TREAT-MENT (Rx)	TREATMENT OF PARTNER	SPECIAL INSTRUCTIONS	PREVENTIVE MEASURES
SYPHILIS (Loues-Treponema pallidum infection)	*Stage 1 (3 weeks post-exposure):* Chancre on penis, anus, vagina, cervix, rectum (disappears without treatment) *Stage 2 (6 weeks post-exposure):* Rash on feet and hands Fever, sore throat, headaches Pains in joints Nausea Flat-topped growths in most areas of the body	Brain damage Insanity Blindness Heart disease Spinal cord damage	2.4 million units Benzathine Penicillin for 1st and 2nd stages	Essential	Use condoms for 1 month	Avoid multiple partners
TRICHOMONIASIS (Trich)	Frothy, thin, greenish vaginal discharge Vulvar itching, pain Frequent urination May be asymptomatic	None	Flagyl 2 mg orally (single dose) Flagyl 500 mg 2 times a day for 5 days	Essential	Use condoms during treatment Avoid alcohol when taking Flagyl Can cause abnormal Pap smears, repeat in 2 to 3 months	Avoid multiple partners
VENEREAL WARTS (Condylomata acuminata)	Dry, fungating wart-like growths on vulva, vagina, cervix, penis Constant discharge Itching	None	Podophyllin liquid or ointment applied to warts (wash off within 4 hours)	When needed	Several treatments per week Use condoms Watch for treatment (podphyllin) poisoning (symptoms: nausea, diarrhea, paralysis, lethargy, coma)	Avoid multiple partners

APPENDIX 1: SELF-BREAST EXAMINATION

Did you examine your breasts this month?

If you didn't, you should. If you don't know how, we'll tell you.

Once a month, while you're taking a shower, and your skin is still wet and slippery, begin:

Keep your fingers flat, and touch every part of each breast. Feel gently for a lump or thickening. After the shower, continue with a more thorough check.

1. Lie down. Put one hand behind your head. With the other hand, fingers flattened, gently feel your breast. Press ever so lightly. Now examine the other breast.

2. This shows you how to check each breast. Begin at the A and follow the arrows, feeling gently for a lump or thickening. Remember to feel all parts of each breast.

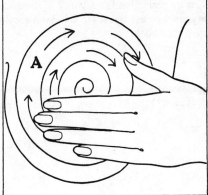

3. Now repeat the same procedure sitting up, with the hand still behind your head (right hand if you're checking the right breast, left hand up in checking the left breast).

Don't be afraid. It's what you don't know that can hurt you.

Most women discover breast changes by themselves. If there is a change, the earlier you find it, the better. But some women don't discover it early enough.

You can avoid that mistake by examining your breasts once a month after your menstrual period. Be sure to continue these checkups after your change of life.

See your doctor as soon as you discover a lump or thickening. In most cases, it turns out to be a perfectly harmless condition. But only the doctor can tell you that for sure. So, for your own peace of mind, see your doctor right away.

Now do your friends a favor: Tell them we'll send free Breast Check booklets to anyone who asks. Just write to your local American Cancer Society Unit; it's in the phone book.

AMERICAN
CANCER
SOCIETY

APPENDIX 2: SUGGESTED FURTHER READING

Barrie Anderson et al., *The Menopause Book* (New York: Hawthorn Books, 1977.)

Lonnie Garfield Barbach, *For Yourself* (New York: Doubleday and Co., 1975.)

The Boston Women's Health Collective, *Our Bodies, Our Selves* rev. and enl. ed. (New York: Simon and Schuster, 1975).

Patricia J. Cooper, ed., *Women's Health & Medical Guide* (Des Moines: Better Homes & Gardens Books, 1981).

Carl Djerassi, *The Politics of Contraception: The Present (vol. 1); The Future (vol. 2),* (Stanford, CA: Stanford Alumni Association, 1979).

Robert A. Hatcher et al., *Contraceptive Technology, 1982–1983* (New York: Irvington Publishers, 1982).

Marion Howard, *Only Human* (New York: The Seabury Press, 1975).

William H. Masters and Virginia E. Johnson, *Human Sexual Response* (Boston: Little Brown, 1966).

Margaret Nofzieger, *A Cooperative Method of Natural Birth Control* (Summertown, Tenn.: The Book Publishing Co., 1976).

Population Information Program, *Population Reports.* Available from The Johns Hopkins University, Hampton House, 624 North Broadway, Baltimore, Maryland 21205. Free.

Barbara Seaman and Gideon Seaman, *Women and The Crisis in Sex Hormones* (New York: Rawson Associates Publishers, 1977).

Felicia Stewart et al., *My Body, My Health* (New York: Bantam Books, 1981).

Task Force on Concerns of Physically Disabled Women, *Toward Intimacy* (New York: Human Science Press, 1977). Available from Reproductive Health Resources, Inc., 1507 21st Street, Suite 100, Sacramento, California 95814.

APPENDIX 3: REFERENCES—FAILURE RATE TABLE

1. B. Vaughn et al., "Contraceptive failure among women in the United States, 1970–1973," *Family Planning Perspectives* 1976:8:81–86.
2. G.S. Bernstein, "Clinical effectiveness of an aerosol contraceptive foam, contraception," 1971:3:1:37–43.
3. J.E. Davis, "Vasectomy," *American Journal of Nursing* 1972:3:509–513.
4. A. Ferrari et al., "The menstrual cycle in women treated with D-Norgestrel 37.5 micrograms in continuous administration," *International Journal of Fertility* 1973:18:133–140.
5. A. Greenspan and R.A. Hatcher, "The prevalence of estrogen use and pregnancy in women using depotmedroxyprogesterone acetate," Unpublished paper, September 1979.
6. F. Guy and M. Guy, The Marutius program in: Uricchio, W.A. and William MK eds. Proceedings of a research conference on natural planning: Washington D.C., Human Life Foundation, 1973, pp. 239–248.
7. A. Ishihama and T. Inoue, "Clinical field test of a new contraceptive vaginal foam tablet," *Contraception* 1972:6:5:401–410.
8. J.A. Johnston, D.B. Roberts, and R.B. Spencer, "A survey evaluation of the efficacy and efficiency of natural family planning services and methods in Australia: Report of a research project," Sydney, Australia, 1978.
9. V.D. Korba and S.R. Paulson, "Five years of fertility control with microdose norgestrel: an updated clinical review," *Journal of Reproductive Medicine* 1974:13:2:71–75.
10. M.E. Lane, R. Arceo, and A.J. Sobrero, "Successful use of the diaphragm and jelly by a young population: Report of a clinical study," *Family Planning Perspectives* 1976:8:81–86.
11. J. Marshall, "Cervical-mucus and basal body temperature method of regulating births: Field Trial," *The Lancet* 1976:2:282.
12. J. Peel, "The Hull family survey," *Journal of Biosocial Science* 1972:4:333–346.
13. F.J. Rice, O. Lanctot, and A.C. Garcia-Deves, "The effectiveness of the sympto-thermal method of natural family planning: An international study." Paper presented at the Scientific Congress held in conjunction with First General Assembly. International Federation of Family Life Promotion, in Cali, Colombia, S.A., 1977.
14. Royal College of General Practitioners, "Oral contraceptives and health: An interim report, (New York: Pitman, 1974).
15. N.B. Ryder, "Contraceptive failure in the United States," *Family Planning Perspectives* 1973:5:133–142.
16. F.D. Scutchfield et al., "Medroxyprogesterone acetate as an injectable female contraceptive," *Contraception* 1971:3:21–35.

17. M.C. Sheps, "An analysis of reproductive patterns in an American isolate," *Population Studies* 1965:19:1:65–76.

18. C. Tietze, "Ranking of contraceptive methods by levels of effectiveness," *Advances in Planned Parenthood* 1971:6:117–126.

19. C. Tietze, H. Lehfeldt, and H.G. Liebmann, "The effectiveness of the cervical cap as a contraceptive method," *American Journal of Obstetrics & Gynecology* 1953:66:904–908.

20. C. Tietze, S. Lewit, "Evaluation of intrauterine devices: Ninth progress report of the Cooperative Statistical Program," *Studies in Family Planning* 1970:7:55:1–40.

21. C. Tietze, S. Lewit, "The IUD and the Pill: Extended use effectiveness," *Family Planning Perspectives* 1971:3:2:54.

22. C. Tietze, S.K. Poleakoff, and J. Rock, "The clinical effectiveness of the rhythm method of contraception," *Fertility and Sterility* 1951:2:5:444–450.

23. M. Vessey and P. Wiggins, "Use-effectiveness of the diaphragm in a selected family planning clinic population," *Contraception* 1974:9:15–21.

24. M. Weissman et al., "Natural family planning in a pacific island community: A Trial of the Ovulation Method in Tonga, 1970–1972," *Lancet* 1972:2:813.

25. C.F. Westoff et al., *Family Growth in Metropolitan America* 1961:363.

26. *World Health Organization Special Programme of Research, Development, and Research Training in Human Reproduction, Seventh Annual Report,* Geneva, November 1978.

APPENDIX 4: GLOSSARY

ABORTION: The termination of a pregnancy.

ABSTINENCE: The practice of not having penis-in-vagina intercourse, although not necessarily avoiding any other types of sexual gratification.

BACKUP METHOD: A second or additional means of birth control.

CERVIX: The entrance to the uterus.

CLITORIS: A small organ located above the outside opening of the woman's vagina and her urinary tract. The clitoris is the most sexually sensitive part of the female body and is the only organ that is capable of leading to orgasm.

COITUS INTERRUPTUS: Another name for the withdrawal method of birth control.

COMBINED BIRTH CONTROL PILL: A pill containing two hormones, estrogen and progestin. These two man-made chemicals, if taken every 24 hours, prevent the release of an egg (ovulation) and the possibility of pregnancy.

CONCEPTION: The joining of sperm and egg which results in a pregnancy.

CONDOM: A rubber sheath that is placed on an erect penis before intercourse. Condoms can be lubricated or non-lubricated, with a tip or without, ribbed or smooth, colored or flesh-toned. Condoms hold semen, preventing it from coming in contact with the vagina.

CONTRACEPTION: Birth control.

CORPUS LUTEUM: A small, yellow hormone-producing lump which forms on the surface of the ovary after ovulation. The corpus luteum produces the hormone progesterone for about 14 days and then disappears leaving only a small, smooth bump on the ovary.

CYSTITIS: An infection of the bladder.

DANGER SIGNALS: Symptoms or side effects resulting from a medication. Danger signals usually alert the patient and his/her doctor to a more serious medical problem. If a danger signal develops, contact your doctor immediately.

DIAPHRAGM: A dome-shaped rubber cap with a flexible rim which is inserted into the vagina before intercourse. Because it covers the cervix, sperm cannot enter the uterine cavity.

DILATION AND CURETTAGE: The process of widening the cervix (dilation) and of scraping (curettage) the uterine cavity. This is often referred to as a "D & C".

DOUCHING: The process of cleansing the vagina by squirting a liquid into the vaginal canal. Because douching changes the normal vaginal environment, it is not recommended as a daily practice.

ECTOPIC PREGNANCY: The implantation of the fertilized egg outside the uterus, usually in the fallopian tubes. Ectopic situations occur in about 1 in 50 to 200 pregnancies and can be extremely dangerous.

EJACULATION: The release of sperm and semen by the penis when a male reaches orgasm. Each time a man ejaculates he releases approximately 400 million sperm.

ESTROGEN: The female sex hormone produced in the ovaries. Estrogens stimulate the female reproductive system, signaling it to begin and maintain its natural cycle. Estrogens are the key ingredient in the combined birth control Pill and often are responsible for the more serious side effects associated with Pill use.

FALLOPIAN TUBES: 2 long, thin tubes connecting the ovaries to the uterus. Conception usually occurs in the fallopian tubes.

FERTILE PERIOD: The time span during a woman's menstrual cycle when she is most likely to get pregnant. This occurs during ovulation, usually around day 14 of a 28-day cycle.

FERTILITY AWARENESS METHODS: Methods of birth control which help a woman determine when during her cycle she is fertile. Fertility awareness methods are based on natural cyclic changes which occur during a menstrual cycle. The basal body temperature method, the calendar method and the cervical mucus method are all fertility awareness methods.

FIRST TRIMESTER: The first 13 weeks of a pregnancy. Start of a pregnancy (gestational stage) is determined from the first day of the last menstrual period.

FSH (FOLLICLE STIMULATING HORMONE): A hormone produced by the pituitary gland which signals the ovary to ripen an egg.

HORMONES: Chemicals in the body which trigger reproductive processes such as ovulation and menstruation.

INTRAUTERINE DEVICE (IUD): A small piece of flexible plastic that is inserted into the uterus. IUDs come in various shapes and sizes. They probably prevent pregnancy by stopping the fertilized egg from being implanted into the wall of the uterus.

LACTATION: The act of breast-feeding.

LH (LUTEINIZING HORMONE): A hormone produced by the pituitary gland which signals the ovary to release an egg.

MASTURBATION: The act of exciting your own genitals strictly for sexual pleasure.

MENSTRUATION: A woman's normal monthly bleeding caused by the uterus shedding its inner lining. Menstruation is also called "Monthly period" and "menses."

MINI-PILL: A pill containing one man-made chemical, progestin. Taking the Mini-Pill every day often prevents ovulation. It also thickens the mucus that is produced in the cervix, making it difficult for the sperm to get into the uterus.

OVARY: An egg-shaped organ which releases an egg each month. There are two ovaries in the female pelvis; each is located at the openned end of the fallopian tubes.

OVULATION: The release of an egg by the ovary. For most women one egg is released about every four weeks, usually on the 14th day of a 28-day cycle.

PAP SMEAR: A routine gynecologic test which detects abnormalities or cancer of the cervix in women. A sample of cells are taken from the cervix during a pelvic examination.

PELVIC INFLAMMATORY DISEASE (PID): Infection of the sex organs, including the uterus (where it is called endometritis), the tubes (where it is called salpingitis), the ovaries, or the pelvic cavity. PID can block the fallopian tubes and lead to infertility.

PREMATURE EJACULATION: The inability to control the timing of ejaculation.

PROGESTERONE: The female sex hormone produced in the corpus luteum. Progesterone is responsible for preparing the uterus for a fertilized egg. It is also produced at very high levels during the first weeks of pregnancy.

PROGESTINS: The term used to describe a variety of man-made hormonal preparations which have some chemical similarities to natural progesterone. Progestins are found in both combined birth control Pills and Mini-Pills.

PROLACTIN: The hormone that stimulates milk production in the breast. Prolactin provides a contraceptive effect by decreasing the level of LH (luteinizing hormone) necessary for ovulation.

SECOND TRIMESTER: Refers to the time period between the 14th and 24th week of pregnancy.

SPERMICIDE: A chemical preparation that kills sperm and partially blocks the opening to the uterus. Foams, jellies, creams, and suppositories are various forms of spermicide.

STERILE: The inability of a man to father a child or of a woman to get pregnant.

STERILIZATION: An operation done to make a man or a woman sterile. Sterilizations should be considered permanent methods of contraception.

TUBAL LIGATION: The operation performed on a woman to make her sterile. This procedure involves tying, cutting, or blocking the fallopian tubes.

UTERUS: A triangular shaped reproductive organ located in the female pelvis which prepares its lining each month for the implantation of a fertilized egg.

VAGINITIS: An inflammation of the vagina, usually caused by a change in the vaginal environment.

VASECTOMY: The operation performed to make a man sterile. This procedure involves tying, cutting or blocking the vas deferens.

WITHDRAWAL: A birth control method whereby the man takes his penis out of the vagina before ejaculation.

APPENDIX 5

REPRODUCTIVE LIFE PLAN

Birth control must fit into your reproductive life plan. Ask yourself these questions to help you work out your personal reproductive life plan:

Would I like to have children one day? _____

Would I like to be married one day? _____

How old would I like to be when I have my first child? _____

How many children would I like to have? _____

How sad would I be if I were not able to have any children _____

How concerned would I be if I were to become pregnant before I were married? _____

If I were to become pregnant before I wanted to become pregnant, would I consider an abortion? _____

Would I like to wait until I'm married to start having sexual intercourse? ___

How many years of formal education would I like to complete? _____

At what point during or after my education would I like to be married? _____

Would I like to work when my children are toddlers? When my children are in their childhood years? When my children are no longer in the home? _____

Of all the things I could do in my life, probably the most important for me to accomplish is this: _____
_____

Children would affect this goal in the following ways: _____
_____

What would it mean to me if my marriage were to end in divorce? _____
_____

Would I like to have intercourse with the person I marry before marriage? __

How does my life plan fit in with my ethical or religious beliefs? _____
_____

How do I feel about having intercourse with someone other than my spouse?

How do I feel about my spouse having intercourse with someone else? _____

How often will I have intercourse? _____

Might I have intercourse with several different partners? _____

REPRODUCTIVE LIFE PLAN

Birth control must fit into your reproductive life plan. Ask yourself these questions to help you work out your personal reproductive life plan:

Would I like to have children one day? _____

Would I like to be married one day? _____

How old would I like to be when I have my first child? _____

How many children would I like to have? _____

How sad would I be if I were not able to have any children _____

How concerned would I be if I were to become pregnant before I were married? _____

If I were to become pregnant before I wanted to become pregnant, would I consider an abortion? _____

Would I like to wait until I'm married to start having sexual intercourse? __

How many years of formal education would I like to complete? __

At what point during or after my education would I like to be married? ___

Would I like to work when my children are toddlers? When my children are in their childhood years? When my children are no longer in the home? _____

Of all the things I could do in my life, probably the most important for me to accomplish is this: _____
_____

Children would affect this goal in the following ways: _____
_____

What would it mean to me if my marriage were to end in divorce? _____
_____

Would I like to have intercourse with the person I marry before marriage? __

How does my life plan fit in with my ethical or religious beliefs? _____
_____

How do I feel about having intercourse with someone other than my spouse?

How do I feel about my spouse having intercourse with someone else? ____

How often will I have intercourse? _____

Might I have intercourse with several different partners? _____

FEELINGS ABOUT BIRTH CONTROL: A SELF-ASSESSMENT QUESTION-NAIRE FOR INDIVIDUALS CONSIDERING USE OF A SPECIFIC METHOD OF BIRTH CONTROL
(for women and men considering their contraceptive options)

BACKGROUND: For each method of birth control there is a rate of failure, or a rate of pregnancies, which may occur even if that method of birth control is used perfectly. Since you will be using your method of birth control to avoid an unplanned pregnancy, you want to get just as low a pregnancy rate as possible. You want to be able to use your method **CORRECTLY** and **CONSISTENTLY** every time. Obviously, the rate of pregnancies, or failure rate, goes up if for any reason you don't use the method or if you fail to use it exactly as it was designed to be used. The following questions were developed to help you decide if the method you are considering is a good choice or a poor choice for you.

METHOD OF BIRTH CONTROL YOU ARE CONSIDERING USING: _____
Have you had problems using this method before? Yes ____ No ____
How long did you use this method? _____

PLEASE ASK YOURSELF THESE QUESTIONS:	YES	NO
Am I afraid of using this method?	——	——
Would I really rather not use this method?	——	——
Will I have trouble remembering to use this method?	——	——
Have I ever become pregnant while using this method?	——	——
Will I have trouble using this method correctly?	——	——
Do I still have unanswered questions about this method?	——	——
Does this method make menstrual periods longer or more painful?	——	——
Does this method cost more than I can afford?	——	——
Is this method known to have serious complications?	——	——
Am I opposed to this method because of any religious beliefs?	——	——
Is my partner opposed to this method?	——	——
Am I using this method without my partner's knowledge?	——	——
Will using this method embarrass my partner?	——	——
Will using this method embarrass me?	——	——
Will I enjoy intercourse less because of this method?	——	——
Will this method interrupt lovemaking?	——	——
Has a nurse or doctor ever told me **NOT** to use this method?	——	——
Is there anything about my personality that could lead me to use this method incorrectly?	——	——

TOTAL NUMBER OF YES ANSWERS: ____

Most individuals will have a few **yes** answers. **Yes** answers mean that potential problems may lie in store. If you have more than a few **yes** responses, you may want to discuss some of these with your physician, counselor, partner, or friend. Talking it over can help you to decide whether to use this method, or how to use it so it will really be effective for you. In general, the more yes answers you have, the less likely you are to use this method consistently and correctly.

FEELINGS ABOUT BIRTH CONTROL: A SELF-ASSESSMENT QUESTION-NAIRE FOR INDIVIDUALS CONSIDERING USE OF A SPECIFIC METHOD OF BIRTH CONTROL
(for women and men considering their contraceptive options)

BACKGROUND: For each method of birth control there is a rate of failure, or a rate of pregnancies, which may occur even if that method of birth control is used perfectly. Since you will be using your method of birth control to avoid an unplanned pregnancy, you want to get just as low a pregnancy rate as possible. You want to be able to use your method **CORRECTLY** and **CONSISTENTLY** every time. Obviously, the rate of pregnancies, or failure rate, goes up if for any reason you don't use the method or if you fail to use it exactly as it was designed to be used. The following questions were developed to help you decide if the method you are considering is a good choice or a poor choice for you.

METHOD OF BIRTH CONTROL YOU ARE CONSIDERING USING: _____
Have you had problems using this method before?   Yes _____   No _____
How long did you use this method? _____

PLEASE ASK YOURSELF THESE QUESTIONS:	**YES**	**NO**
Am I afraid of using this method?	____	____
Would I really rather not use this method?	____	____
Will I have trouble remembering to use this method?	____	____
Have I ever become pregnant while using this method?	____	____
Will I have trouble using this method correctly?	____	____
Do I still have unanswered questions about this method?	____	____
Does this method make menstrual periods longer or more painful?	____	____
Does this method cost more than I can afford?	____	____
Is this method known to have serious complications?	____	____
Am I opposed to this method because of any religious beliefs?	____	____
Is my partner opposed to this method?	____	____
Am I using this method without my partner's knowledge?	____	____
Will using this method embarrass my partner?	____	____
Will using this method embarrass me?	____	____
Will I enjoy intercourse less because of this method?	____	____
Will this method interrupt lovemaking?	____	____
Has a nurse or doctor ever told me **NOT** to use this method?	____	____
Is there anything about my personality that could lead me to use this method incorrectly?	____	____

TOTAL NUMBER OF YES ANSWERS: _____

Most individuals will have a few **yes** answers. **Yes** answers mean that potential problems may lie in store. If you have more than a few **yes** responses, you may want to discuss some of these with your physician, counselor, partner, or friend. Talking it over can help you to decide whether to use this method, or how to use it so it will really be effective for you. In general, *the more yes answers you have, the less likely you are to use this method consistently and correctly.*

FEELINGS ABOUT BIRTH CONTROL: A SELF-ASSESSMENT QUESTION-NAIRE FOR INDIVIDUALS CONSIDERING USE OF A SPECIFIC METHOD OF BIRTH CONTROL
(for women and men considering their contraceptive options)

BACKGROUND: For each method of birth control there is a rate of failure, or a rate of pregnancies, which may occur even if that method of birth control is used perfectly. Since you will be using your method of birth control to avoid an unplanned pregnancy, you want to get just as low a pregnancy rate as possible. You want to be able to use your method **CORRECTLY** and **CONSISTENTLY** every time. Obviously, the rate of pregnancies, or failure rate, goes up if for any reason you don't use the method or if you fail to use it exactly as it was designed to be used. The following questions were developed to help you decide if the method you are considering is a good choice or a poor choice for you.

METHOD OF BIRTH CONTROL YOU ARE CONSIDERING USING: _____
Have you had problems using this method before?   Yes _____   No _____
How long did you use this method? _____

PLEASE ASK YOURSELF THESE QUESTIONS:	YES	NO
Am I afraid of using this method?	___	___
Would I really rather not use this method?	___	___
Will I have trouble remembering to use this method?	___	___
Have I ever become pregnant while using this method?	___	___
Will I have trouble using this method correctly?	___	___
Do I still have unanswered questions about this method?	___	___
Does this method make menstrual periods longer or more painful?	___	___
Does this method cost more than I can afford?	___	___
Is this method known to have serious complications?	___	___
Am I opposed to this method because of any religious beliefs?	___	___
Is my partner opposed to this method?	___	___
Am I using this method without my partner's knowledge?	___	___
Will using this method embarrass my partner?	___	___
Will using this method embarrass me?	___	___
Will I enjoy intercourse less because of this method?	___	___
Will this method interrupt lovemaking?	___	___
Has a nurse or doctor ever told me **NOT** to use this method?	___	___
Is there anything about my personality that could lead me to use this method incorrectly?	___	___

TOTAL NUMBER OF YES ANSWERS: ___

Most individuals will have a few **yes** answers. **Yes** answers mean that potential problems may lie in store. If you have more than a few **yes** responses, you may want to discuss some of these with your physician, counselor, partner, or friend. Talking it over can help you to decide whether to use this method, or how to use it so it will really be effective for you. In general, the more yes answers you have, the less likely you are to use this method consistently and correctly.

FEELINGS ABOUT BIRTH CONTROL: A SELF-ASSESSMENT QUESTIONNAIRE FOR INDIVIDUALS CONSIDERING USE OF A SPECIFIC METHOD OF BIRTH CONTROL
(for women and men considering their contraceptive options)

BACKGROUND: For each method of birth control there is a rate of failure, or a rate of pregnancies, which may occur even if that method of birth control is used perfectly. Since you will be using your method of birth control to avoid an unplanned pregnancy, you want to get just as low a pregnancy rate as possible. You want to be able to use your method **CORRECTLY** and **CONSISTENTLY** every time. Obviously, the rate of pregnancies, or failure rate, goes up if for any reason you don't use the method or if you fail to use it exactly as it was designed to be used. The following questions were developed to help you decide if the method you are considering is a good choice or a poor choice for you.

METHOD OF BIRTH CONTROL YOU ARE CONSIDERING USING: _____

Have you had problems using this method before?   Yes ____   No ____

How long did you use this method?   _____

PLEASE ASK YOURSELF THESE QUESTIONS:	YES	NO
Am I afraid of using this method?	____	____
Would I really rather not use this method?	____	____
Will I have trouble remembering to use this method?	____	____
Have I ever become pregnant while using this method?	____	____
Will I have trouble using this method correctly?	____	____
Do I still have unanswered questions about this method?	____	____
Does this method make menstrual periods longer or more painful?	____	____
Does this method cost more than I can afford?	____	____
Is this method known to have serious complications?	____	____
Am I opposed to this method because of any religious beliefs?	____	____
Is my partner opposed to this method?	____	____
Am I using this method without my partner's knowledge?	____	____
Will using this method embarrass my partner?	____	____
Will using this method embarrass me?	____	____
Will I enjoy intercourse less because of this method?	____	____
Will this method interrupt lovemaking?	____	____
Has a nurse or doctor ever told me **NOT** to use this method?	____	____
Is there anything about my personality that could lead me to use this method incorrectly?	____	____

TOTAL NUMBER OF YES ANSWERS: ____

Most individuals will have a few **yes** answers. **Yes** answers mean that potential problems may lie in store. If you have more than a few **yes** responses, you may want to discuss some of these with your physician, counselor, partner, or friend. Talking it over can help you to decide whether to use this method, or how to use it so it will really be effective for you. In general, the more yes answers you have, the less likely you are to use this method consistently and correctly.

INDEX

PLEASE USE THIS FORM TO ORDER
ORDERING INSTRUCTIONS

Individuals must include payment with order. This entire form (or a copy) must be returned.

Libraries and institutions may send official purchase orders with this order form or copy attached.

All sales final. No returns. NOTE: On bookstore purchases for class adoption our standard returns policy applies.

> Please send this order form to IRVINGTON
> PUBLISHERS, DEPT. CTM, 551 FIFTH
> AVENUE, NEW YORK, NY 10176

If payment accompanies your order and shipment cannot be made within 30 days, payment will be refunded upon request.

> *Clinic and M.D. Discount*
> *It's Your Choice* is available to Clinics, M.D.'s and any others providing health counseling services at special discounts for orders of 50 copies or more. To obtain a discount schedule, please write to Special Sales Dept., Irvington Publishers, Inc., 551 Fifth Ave., New York, N.Y. 10176.

Qty.	Title	Price
_____	It's Your Choice	$ 7.95
_____	Sexually Transmitted Diseases	$ 8.95
_____	Passport to Good Health	$ 8.95
_____	Managing Contraceptive Pill Patients	$ 8.95
_____	Nutrition in Health Care	$ 8.95
_____	Managing Patients With Intrauterine Devices	$ 8.95
_____	Abortion Services Handbook	$ 7.95
_____	My Body, My Health	$ 9.95
_____	Nuestros Cuerpos, Nuestras Vidas (Our Bodies, Our Selves) (in Spanish)	$ 5.00
_____	Nurses in Family Planning	paper $12.95
_____		cloth $24.50
	Contraceptive Technology, 11th Edition, 1982-1983	
_____		paper $9.95
_____		cloth $18.95
_____	Contraceptive Technology, 9th Edition, 1978-79	$ 3.95
_____	Contraceptive Technology, 10th Edition, 1980-81 with special section on Teenage Contraception	$ 4.50

Please complete this form on reverse side.

PLEASE PHOTOCOPY THIS FORM OR CUT ALONG THIS LINE AND MAIL

Individual Chapters: It's Your Choice

Chap. # & Title	Price/Chap	Qty.	Total
_____	_____	____	____
_____	_____	____	____
_____	_____	____	____
_____	_____	____	____
_____	_____	____	____
_____	_____	____	____
_____	_____	____	____

Cost of items $_____

NY State residents
add appropriate
sales tax (NYC 8½%) $_____

postage & handling 15% $_____
(minimum $1.25)

Total $_____

____ Enclosed is my check
or money order
____ Attached is Purchase Order (institutions only)

Ship to: Name _____

Address _____

City _____

State _____ Zip _____

Please send: (Qty.)

____ Additional Order Forms   ____ Sociology Catalog(s)
____ Psychology Catalog(s)   ____ Health & Human Services Catalog(s)

Standing Order   (Applies only to libraries and institutions.)

Please enter my standing order for each issue of *Contraceptive Technology* every two years upon publication.
____ paper edition. ____ cloth edition.

Prices may vary outside U.S.
Prices subject to change without notice.

PLEASE USE THIS FORM TO ORDER
ORDERING INSTRUCTIONS

Individuals must include payment with order. This entire form (or a copy) must be returned.

Libraries and institutions may send official purchase orders with this order form or copy attached.

All sales final. No returns. NOTE: On bookstore purchases for class adoption our standard returns policy applies.

> Please send this order form to IRVINGTON PUBLISHERS, DEPT. CTM, 551 FIFTH AVENUE, NEW YORK, NY 10176

If payment accompanies your order and shipment cannot be made within 30 days, payment will be refunded upon request.

> *Clinic and M.D. Discount*
> *It's Your Choice* is available to Clinics, M.D.'s and any others providing health counseling services at special discounts for orders of 50 copies or more. To obtain a discount schedule, please write to Special Sales Dept., Irvington Publishers, Inc., 551 Fifth Ave., New York, N.Y. 10176.

Qty.	Title	Price
____	It's Your Choice	$ 7.95
____	Sexually Transmitted Diseases	$ 8.95
____	Passport to Good Health	$ 8.95
____	Managing Contraceptive Pill Patients	$ 8.95
____	Nutrition in Health Care	$ 8.95
____	Managing Patients With Intrauterine Devices	$ 8.95
____	Abortion Services Handbook	$ 7.95
____	My Body, My Health	$ 9.95
____	Nuestros Cuerpos, Nuestras Vidas (Our Bodies, Our Selves) (in Spanish)	$ 5.00
____	Nurses in Family Planning	paper $12.95
____		cloth $24.50
	Contraceptive Technology, 11th Edition, 1982-1983	
____		paper $9.95
____		cloth $18.95
____	Contraceptive Technology, 9th Edition, 1978-79	$ 3.95
____	Contraceptive Technology, 10th Edition, 1980-81 with special section on Teenage Contraception	$ 4.50

Please complete this form on reverse side.

Individual Chapters: It's Your Choice

Chap. # & Title	Price/Chap	Qty.	Total
_____	_____	___	___
_____	_____	___	___
_____	_____	___	___
_____	_____	___	___
_____	_____	___	___
_____	_____	___	___

Cost of items $_____

NY State residents
add appropriate
sales tax (NYC 8½%) $_____

postage & handling 15% $_____
(minimum $1.25)

Total $_____

_____ Enclosed is my check
        or money order
_____ Attached is Purchase Order (institutions only)

Ship to: Name _____

            Address _____

            City _____

            State _____ Zip _____

Please send: (Qty.)

_____ Additional Order Forms   _____ Sociology Catalog(s)
_____ Psychology Catalog(s)   _____ Health & Human Services Catalog(s)

Standing Order   (Applies only to libraries and institutions.)

Please enter my standing order for each issue of *Contraceptive Technology* every two years upon publication.
_____ paper edition. _____ cloth edition.

Prices may vary outside U.S.
Prices subject to change without notice.